Managing Healthcare Ethically

Managing Healthcare Ethically

THIRD EDITION

VOLUME 2

Organizational Concerns

ACHE Management Series

William A. Nelson | Paul B. Hofmann | Editors

Your board, staff, or clients may also benefit from this book's insight. For information on quantity discounts, contact the Health Administration Press Marketing Manager at (312) 424-9450.

This publication is intended to provide accurate and authoritative information in regard to the subject matter covered. It is sold, or otherwise provided, with the understanding that the publisher is not engaged in rendering professional services. If professional advice or other expert assistance is required, the services of a competent professional should be sought.

The statements and opinions contained in this book are strictly those of the authors and do not represent the official positions of the American College of Healthcare Executives or the Foundation of the American College of Healthcare Executives.

26 25 24 23 22   5 4 3 2 1

Library of Congress Cataloging-in-Publication Data
Names: Nelson, William A., editor. | Hofmann, Paul B., 1941– editor.
Title: Managing healthcare ethically / William A. Nelson, Paul B. Hofmann, editors.
Other titles: Management series (Ann Arbor, Mich.)
Description: Third edition. | Chicago, IL : Health Administration Press, [2022] | Series: HAP/ACHE management series | Includes bibliographical references. | Contents: v. 1. Leadership roles and responsibilities — v. 2. Organizational concerns — v. 3. Clinical challenges. | Summary: "This book discusses the numerous and complex issues that healthcare executives encounter every day as an intrinsic part of organizational life"— Provided by publisher.
Identifiers: LCCN 2021023677 (print) | LCCN 2021023678 (ebook) | ISBN 9781640552500 (v. 1 ; paperback ; alk. paper) | ISBN 9781640552555 (v. 2 ; paperback ; alk. paper) | ISBN 9781640552609 (v. 3 ; paperback ; alk. paper) | ISBN 9781640552470 (v. 1 ; epub) | ISBN 9781640552487 (v. 1 ; mobi) | ISBN 9781640552524 (v. 2 ; epub) | ISBN 9781640552531 (v. 2 ; mobi) | ISBN 9781640552579 (v. 3 ; epub) | ISBN 9781640552586 (v. 3 ; mobi)
Subjects: MESH: Health Services Administration—ethics | Leadership
Classification: LCC RA971 (print) | LCC RA971 (ebook) | NLM W 84.1 | DDC 362.1068—dc23
LC record available at https://lccn.loc.gov/2021023677
LC ebook record available at https://lccn.loc.gov/2021023678

The paper used in this publication meets the minimum requirements of American National Standard for Information Sciences—Permanence of Paper for Printed Library Materials, ANSI Z39.48-1984. ♾™

Acquisitions editor: Jennette McClain; Project manager: Andrew Baumann; Cover designer: Book Buddy Media; Layout: Integra

Found an error or a typo? We want to know! Please e-mail it to hapbooks@ache.org, mentioning the book's title and putting "Book Error" in the subject line.

For photocopying and copyright information, please contact Copyright Clearance Center at www.copyright.com or at (978) 750-8400.

Health Administration Press
A division of the Foundation of the American
    College of Healthcare Executives
300 S. Riverside Plaza, Suite 1900
Chicago, IL 60606-6698
(312) 424-2800

Contents

Foreword

As HEALTHCARE EXECUTIVES, WE regularly face a range of issues in which ethics plays an important role, from determining what services are needed in the communities we serve, to always maintaining good financial stewardship and delivering the best care for patients, their families and your employees.

The American College of Healthcare Executives has made an unwavering commitment to act in ways that merit the trust, confidence and respect of our members, our profession and the general public. We believe all healthcare leaders have a professional obligation to create an ethical culture within the organizations they lead. To this end, we provide our members with several resources that serve as a touchstone in times and situations of uncertainty. The "Healthcare Management Ethics" column in *Healthcare Executive*, ACHE's official magazine, has been a key component of our ethics resources since it became a part of the magazine in 1992.

The editors of this new edition, William A. Nelson, PhD, HFACHE, and Paul B. Hofmann, DrPH, LFACHE, have regularly contributed to the column for more than 20 years and are recognized experts in healthcare management ethics. The columns they chose for this second volume of *Managing Healthcare Ethically* focus on issues that affect policies and management within healthcare organizations. An organization's ability to achieve its full potential as an ethically aligned entity depends on the motivation, skills and practices of each individual within the organization, beginning with the C-suite and extending to all front-line workers and support staff. The columns selected for this new edition are meant to guide leaders through the creation of an ethical culture and the fundamental components that serve as the foundation for an organization's ethical framework.

I have personally known Bill and Paul for many years and am familiar with their great work in the field of healthcare management ethics. I am grateful for their adept curation in this new edition. Their wisdom, along with that of the other column contributors, has served as an indispensable source of guidance for ACHE members and healthcare leaders everywhere.

Implementing and improving an ethical organizational culture is not easy; it takes time and it requires intentional leadership. As you integrate ethics into your organization, please remember that ACHE is here to support you and your work.

Deborah J. Bowen, FACHE, CAE
President and CEO
American College of Healthcare Executives

Acknowledgments

WE WANT TO EXPRESS our appreciation to the many authors who have contributed to this book. Their efforts were essential to this edition, as they were to the two previous editions published by Health Administration Press in 2001 and 2010.

We also want to acknowledge the editors of the American College of Healthcare Executive (ACHE) publications that continue to publish articles on ethical topics. These articles are as vital to the leaders of today's healthcare organizations as they are to the educators preparing the leaders of tomorrow.

We would like to express our sincere gratitude to the Health Administration Press team, in particular Jennette McClain for her ongoing encouragement and support throughout the process of publishing this book and Andrew Baumann for his editing assistance.

Finally, we thank Deborah J. Bowen, FACHE, CAE, president and CEO of ACHE, for her unwavering commitment and leadership in supporting the essential role of ethics in the delivery of healthcare and in the education of healthcare executives.

Introduction

THIS IS THE SECOND of three volumes that constitute the third edition of *Managing Healthcare Ethically*, which builds on the two previous editions published by Health Administration Press in 2001 and 2010. The first volume of the third edition concentrates on the skill set and personal attributes executives need to successfully align their organizational and professional ethical values in the life of their organization. It also provides insights to assist executives when confronting challenges created by the ethical issues they encounter. The third volume of the third edition addresses ethical challenges related to clinical care. Like the other two volumes, this one gathers selected columns originally written for American College of Healthcare Executives publications, adds some provocative discussion questions, and offers other material useful for teaching purposes.

Here we focus on an array of organizational ethical challenges. Organizational ethics, unlike clinical ethics, focuses on decisions and actions taken by individuals or groups of people—for example, governing boards and committees—working on behalf of a healthcare organization. These decisions and actions seek to integrate the organization's mission and ethical values into its overall structure, culture, policy, and practices. Therefore, the columns included in this volume reflect the need for clear policies and guidelines that foster and ensure an ethically grounded organization.

Organizational ethics can also be used to establish both management and clinical ethical standards of practice. The columns selected for this volume also include a discussion of how ethics committees are evolving from their traditional role of focusing on clinical issues to the importance of having readily available and effective ethics resources to address organizational ethics challenges.

Instructor Resources

This book's instructor resources include PowerPoint slides, case studies, and lists of selected ethics center websites and selected ethics journals.

For the most up-to-date information about this book and its instructor resources, go to ache.org/HAP and browse for the book's title, author name, or order code (24381).

This book's instructor resources are available to instructors who adopt this book for use in their course. For access information, please e-mail hapbooks@ache.org.

The Impending Physician Shortage

Richard A. Culbertson, PhD

DARRELL G. KIRCH, MD, CEO of the Association of American Medical Colleges, Washington, D.C., has defined physician shortages in the United States as not simply an economic issue but a moral issue. It is a continuing source of surprise that the United States should continue to experience physician shortages given its reputation as an educational magnet to the world. An AAMC report, *The Complexities of Physician Supply and Demand From 2016 to 2030: 2018 Update*, shows 51,680 individuals applied to U.S. medical schools, with 22,388 matriculating—41 percent gaining admission.

Perhaps these figures would not seem troubling were there neither a deficit in the number of practicing physicians, nor one projected in the future. The AAMC 2018 projection suggests that in 2030 the U.S. will experience a physician deficit, ranging from 43,000 to 121,000 physicians at the peak of the baby boom retirement. Contributing factors include increased patient demand and diminished physician supply resulting from the retirement of current practitioners. This shortage will be more acute, it is argued, in the less lucrative primary care disciplines.

This report has been controversial, with critics arguing that the problem is the poor use of physician time on nonclinical tasks and changing work hours expectations of younger physicians.

Geographic and specialty maldistribution also are suggested as root causes. Ezekiel J. Emanuel, MD, PhD, vice provost for Global Initiatives, the Diane v.S. Levy and Robert M. Levy University Professor, and chairman of the Department of Medical Ethics and Health Policy at the University of Pennsylvania, has been a vocal critic of the more dire projections of a shortage that is already in the making.

PHYSICIANS TRAINED ABROAD AS A FORM OF SOLUTION

However one views the current and future availability of physicians, there is no question that the reliance on physicians educated outside the United States has prevented the situation from becoming more alarming. The U.S. Department of Health and Human Services reported in 2016 that approximately one quarter of all active practicing physicians in the U.S. received their medical degrees from nations other than the U.S. or Canada.

Aaron Carrol, MD, professor of pediatrics at Indiana University School of Medicine, noted in a November 2016 article in *The New York Times* that the U.S. has fewer practicing physicians per 1,000 people than 23 of the 28 Organization for Economic Cooperation and Development industrialized nations. The U.S. ranking for primary care physicians is only slightly higher at 24 of 28 OECD nations.

International medical graduates have been viewed as a vital, albeit partial, solution to access and distribution issues as they are more likely to practice primary care than to specialize. In addition, their willingness to practice in rural and urban locations that are underserved by other physicians is a distinct contribution to the U.S. system. Recent political focus on the revision of immigration laws in the United States has refocused attention on this issue, as highly skilled workers are viewed as desirable from an immigration perspective.

PROBLEMS FOR NATIONS OF ORIGIN

Professional migration of highly educated individuals from developing to developed countries helps increase the supply of a skilled workforce in high-income countries, but it is viewed as a serious constraint on the development of poor countries.

This can be especially troubling in the realm of healthcare. Paul Edward Farmer, MD, PhD, Kolokotrones University Professor of Global Health and Social Medicine, Harvard Medical School, has argued that a population's poor health impedes economic growth. The focus of concern is on impoverished nations, particularly those in sub-Saharan Africa. Fifty nations in the world have no medical school at all and are in the vulnerable position of importing physicians out of necessity.

The impact of physician out-migration on source countries is mixed. The clearly negative consequence is an increased shortage of physicians resulting in fewer available health services. The transfer of these skills from the source country might be viewed as a subsidy of sorts to the wealthier country and a reversal of usual economics.

There also are some benefits to the source country. Remittances back to the families or governments of these nations confer direct economic benefit. In the unusual case in which a physician returns to his or her country of origin, significant skills and experience will be gained. China, India and the Philippines have used the export of physicians as an economic strategy, and the United Kingdom has recognized this by exempting these nations from controls to discourage emigration to the U.K. from vulnerable countries.

THE WORLD HEALTH ORGANIZATION POLICY STATEMENT

Julio Frenk, MD, president of the University of Miami, identified the gaps and inequities in health between and within countries in a 2010 article in *The Lancet*. He pointed to new infectious, environmental and behavioral threats superimposed on rapid demographic and epidemiological transitions. He also noted common themes across all societies, notably a significant increase in chronic conditions and patients becoming more proactive in health-seeking behavior.

In response to these considerations, the World Health Organization in 2010 adopted a Code of Conduct on the International Recruitment of Health Personnel. This voluntary policy statement asks member nations to refrain from active recruitment of health professionals from countries with personnel shortages.

THE AUTONOMY OF PHYSICIANS IN A GLOBAL LABOR MARKET

Physicians seek training in the U.S. and other developed countries for learning opportunities that are unavailable to them in their home nations. This may be due to limited availability of capable faculty to instruct, or from a lack of technologies readily available in more affluent nations. In the course of training, economic opportunities may present themselves that are better than in the physician's country of origin. A classic component of the concept of physician autonomy has been the right of the physician to determine locus of practice and specialty based on training. Should this choice be limited in the case of internationally trained physicians?

GUIDANCE FROM ACHE'S *CODE OF ETHICS*

ACHE's *Code of Ethics* stipulates that the healthcare executive shall "Work to support access to healthcare services for all people." As executives, our assessment of our community is routinely defined as a geographic entity, and healthcare is famously seen as local in nature. To satisfy the challenge of the *Code*, "to participate in public dialogue on healthcare issues . . . ," one must adopt a broader perspective on the problem of physician migration that transcends local and national boundaries.

In the present, an ethical executive will hire or encourage the hiring on merit of the most competent physician available for the benefit of patients served, without consideration of his or her nation of origin within the context of immigration laws. However, the long-term problem of a U.S. physician shortage requires policy solutions that will allow the United States to achieve self-sufficiency in ensuring adequate physician supply for its health needs. This could be addressed in a variety of ways, including physician extenders, technological advances and improved organization of care.

Policy goals that executives might consider include advocacy for expanded medical school opportunities for both allopathic and osteopathic physicians. Health systems such as Geisinger, Danville, Pennsylvania; Kaiser Permanente, Oakland, California; and Carilion Clinic, Roanoke, Virginia, have already moved in this direction by establishing medical schools. This might eventually allow the training of medical students in the U.S. to return to their nations of origin.

The U.S. educates a significant number of foreign students in engineering and science but not in medicine. Revising caps on residency funding through Medicare established in the Balanced Budget Act of 1997 would further relieve the shortfall of residency opportunities for U.S. medical graduates. Only through these broader policy initiatives can an ethical resolution to professional migration be attained.

Originally published in the November/December 2018 issue of *Healthcare Executive* magazine.

Discussion Questions

A number of high-income countries have built hospitals and sent physicians to low- and middle-income countries to help train the trainers in an effort to reduce the volume of physicians immigrating to the United States. However, given our

(continued)

country's dependency on foreign-trained clinicians, these worthy efforts exacerbate our physician shortage problem. Other than building more medical schools in the United States, revising the caps on residency funding, and increasing the capacity of existing schools, what other ethically acceptable options might be considered?

Given that most healthcare executives may already feel over-extended, offer some thoughts about when and how this dilemma can be addressed.

Ethical Community Engagement: Lessons Learned

Richard A. Culbertson, PhD

ACHE's *CODE OF ETHICS* devotes a full section to "The Healthcare Executive's Responsibilities to Community and Society." The first of these duties, outlined in Section V of the code, is the mandate to "work to identify and meet the healthcare needs of the community." While it is clearly ethical to meet these needs, a healthcare executive may wonder: What is the most ethical way to identify the community's needs?

In answering this question, it is useful to look at the evolution of research ethics with respect to the community. The National Center for Bioethics in Research and Health Care at Tuskegee University has identified trust as the key issue that stands between researchers and the people of a community, according to the center's "Ethics Across Generations" course, held in April 2018. This is no less true for executives, although their goal of research for the sake of effective program development is different from the pursuit of scientific discovery.

In light of the renewed emphasis in the field on eliminating health disparities, executives and researchers alike have devoted increased resources to addressing these concerns. Writing in an October 10, 2019, issue of *The New York Times*, Peter Goodman profiles the Healthcare Anchor Network of 45 health systems, which seeks to invest in local communities to achieve improved health of community residents.

The article illustrates how Kaiser Permanente sought community input for a new medical campus in the Los Angeles neighborhoods of Crenshaw and Baldwin Village. The need for a medical campus was clear given that for many of the area's residents, the nearest hospital was a 25-minute drive away. Yet, when asked what the community desired, its members responded "jobs"—an answer that might address health disparities through provision of steady incomes, but certainly goes beyond the usual scope of medical services. Kaiser Permanente addressed this community desire in part by devoting a portion of construction funds to female- and minority-owned businesses and workers. This is one example of how healthcare organizations can seek community input and then reasonably respond to that input to build trust and meet needs.

ETHICAL ENGAGEMENT: HARD, BUT NECESSARY WORK

As much as health systems have evolved to adopt new approaches to community partnerships, researchers have confronted similar obstacles in ensuring the community's needs are being considered. In his book *Ethics in Health Services Management*, Kurt Darr of The George Washington University writes that the "respect for persons principle" mandates health administrators are obligated to protect and preserve individual autonomy (self-determination) and the trust of those affected by managerial decisions.

The world of research has not always been as progressive in its view of the community's role in research efforts. Community members in research studies have traditionally been referred to as "subjects." The term implies that the investigator conducting the study is accorded greater power in a relationship through her or his professional expertise. One of the most egregious historical examples of how this power has been exploited—with devastating results—is the infamous Tuskegee syphilis study, which ran from 1932 to 1972 with funding provided by the Centers for Disease Control and

Prevention. The aim of the study was to assess the effects of untreated syphilis infecting adult males. The subjects of the study, African-American men, were not informed of the existence of therapies, and were actually told that they were receiving treatment. Public outcry in 1972 led to congressional hearings and, ultimately, a formal apology in 1997 by then President Bill Clinton. The eventual result was the requirement throughout the healthcare industry for informed consent in both patient care and research.

In patient care settings, providers and executives now speak of the patient's essential role as being a "partner" in her or his healthcare. The language in the field has evolved to reflect this changed thinking. For example, it is no longer considered appropriate to speak of patient "compliance" in the care process. Rather, the term "adherence" is preferred, as this reflects patients' autonomy and the necessity of their willing cooperation in maintaining their health. While compliance is passive on the part of the patient, adherence means willing partnership with the healthcare team and greater outcomes and benefit to the patient as a result.

The WK Kellogg Foundation Community Health Scholars Program defines community-based participatory research as "a collaborative approach to research that equitably involves all partners in the research process and recognizes the unique strengths that each brings." Terence Gipson from the University of Oklahoma Hudson College of Public Health refers to community-based participatory research as the "gold standard" of participatory research. He argues that community participation should address disparities in opportunities, conditions and outcomes across disadvantaged communities that are directly reflected in poor health status. Unlike traditional research that is investigator initiated, community-based participatory research begins with a topic of importance to the community and combines knowledge with action. Ultimately, it aims to achieve social change to improve health outcomes and eliminate health disparities. At that point, the interests of the community, the researcher and the health executive are in accord—an ideal situation.

WHAT DOES THE COMMUNITY WANT FROM RESEARCH?

Benjamin Springgate, MD, and his research team at Louisiana State University and the University of California, Los Angeles, have concluded that community research participants want several key items from their participation that historically have not been part of traditional investigator-driven research. One item is inclusion in research topic selection and project design.

In working with a community group in Los Angeles, the researchers noted an expressed desire by community members for improved information about the mentally ill that might in turn lead to creation of services for these persons and preventive services for the community. Involvement of community members to monitor progress throughout the study was deemed essential. At the study's conclusion, a reporting of the results to participants was most essential to confirm respect for the contribution of study participants.

LESSONS FOR THE HEALTHCARE EXECUTIVE

In her "Perspectives" column in the March/April 2019 issue of *Healthcare Executive*, ACHE President/CEO Deborah J. Bowen, FACHE, CAE, notes the importance of the guidance of ACHE's *Code of Ethics*, especially in "transformational times," stating that our concept of stakeholders has expanded to "the wider community and even society." A similar broadening of vision is underway in the research community. Above all, the "respect for persons" ethical principle demands that trust be established and sustained between researcher, practitioner and community. This requires a good faith demonstration of community involvement in the design and development of a research project from formulation through completion. Finally, no study or project is final until results are shared with the community in recognition of its invaluable participation. Transparency is key.

Originally published in the January/February 2020 issue of *Healthcare Executive* magazine.

Discussion Questions

Establishing and maintaining the community's trust in its institutional provider, including its research activities, is the cornerstone of the author's column. Describe one or two ways this goal could be accomplished in addition to those referenced in the article.

Actively engaging the community in the types of activities highlighted by the author has obvious advantages for the reasons mentioned. However, what practical steps could be taken to determine whether community engagement has actually been successful or made an impact?

The Myth of Comprehensive Policies

Paul B. Hofmann, DrPH, LFACHE

THE IMPORTANCE OF HAVING appropriate policies is undeniable. No one disputes the value of proper policies to maintain consistent processes, promote professional practices and comply with The Joint Commission and regulatory requirements. Similarly, there is no debate that policies should always be consistent with the organization's mission and values.

Everyone also agrees healthcare organizations have an ethical and fiduciary responsibility to establish and implement effective policies to optimize behavior by their staff members. The ultimate goal is to apply policies that serve the best interests of patients and their families by providing clear and sound guidance to those committed to their welfare.

Model policies covering most areas of clinical and business activity have existed for decades. New ones are regularly developed and carefully crafted in response to recommendations by staff, governmental agencies, medical societies, hospital associations and other bodies.

Unfortunately, the mere existence of appropriate policies often produces a false sense of organizational security. Although creating and distributing such policies are obviously the first logical steps, they are not enough. Too many clinical and management leaders erroneously assume the creation and distribution of policies represent the two most crucial actions to take. However, unless four additional imperatives are fulfilled, there is a high likelihood that staff and patients will be severely compromised. Not only will inconsistent performance be inevitable but a real potential exists for substantial legal liability.

BEYOND CREATING AND DISTRIBUTING POLICIES

Most executives would agree that implementation of effective policies requires more than simply composing and disseminating these documents. What they may be less likely to demonstrate in practice is what 100 percent adherence demands:

1. Providing intensive education, followed by an evaluation to confirm that those responsible for conforming to the policies understand their content and the rationale for their application
2. Monitoring compliance to determine (a) the frequency, type, source and possible patterns of noncompliance and (b) the reasons for either legitimate exceptions or inappropriate noncompliance
3. Addressing issues of noncompliance by designing and implementing interventions to reduce and prevent their incidence
4. Regularly reviewing and revising policies to ensure they remain current, pragmatic and responsive to internal and external requirements

According to The Joint Commission, "The human element is the most critical factor in any process, determining whether the right things are done correctly. The best policies and procedures for minimizing risks in the environment where care, treatment, and services are provided are meaningless if staff, licensed independent practitioners, if applicable, students, and volunteers do not know and understand them well enough to perform them properly."

EXAMPLES OF LAUDABLE INTENTIONS
BUT INCONSISTENT RESULTS

People who provide healthcare, and those who receive and pay for care, are justifiably concerned about clinical errors and patient safety. Based on the expanding literature and ubiquitous educational programs, as well as the continuing pressure to reduce mistakes, every institutional provider has adopted comprehensive policies, supplemented by detailed procedures. And yet, no one would assert that these documents alone have been the reason for our progress.

Much of the impressive progress in patient safety has been due to replicating best practices described by the growing number of leaders in this field. Consequently, major initiatives have produced significant and commendable improvements, but even patients in the best institutions with well-earned local, state and national awards still suffer from preventable mistakes.

For example, this year two nationally prominent hospitals with enviable safety records were subject to litigation, in part because they allegedly failed to follow their own policies. In one case, an unattended patient whose high risk of falling was well documented fell and suffered a subdural hematoma. In the second case, a patient's healthy kidney was removed instead of the kidney with a malignancy. Thus, as medication and transfusion errors, healthcare-associated infections, wrong-site surgery, patient falls, inadequate communication of critical results and comparable problems continue to occur, public confidence in our hospitals will remain justifiably uneven.

Last year, researchers funded by the Robert Wood Johnson Foundation reported in *Health Affairs* that *adverse events occur in a third of hospital admissions*. And according to a report issued in January by the inspector general of the Department of Health and Human Services, even after hospitals investigated preventable injuries and infections, they "made few changes to policies or practices" to prevent repetition of the adverse events.

So what should be done to answer this indictment? Certainly, at the very least, after completion of a root cause analysis and/or failure mode and effects analysis, institutions should reexamine their policies and practices. Once essential revisions are made, only then does the real work begin:

- The updated policies must be clear and be followed uniformly.
- Staff members must understand how much discretion, if any, can be used in the policies' application.
- The importance of correct documentation must be emphasized.
- A reliable system must be in place for monitoring compliance.
- Policy violations, particularly those affecting patient care, must be reported and dealt with promptly.

Of course, policies alone are not sufficient. If the underlying systems-based causes of errors and associated vulnerabilities are not identified and corrected, potential hazards will still place patients in jeopardy. Policies must go beyond warning or admonishing staff to try harder or to be more careful if these policies are to play a real role in sustained improvement.

Nonpunitive and just cultures have contributed to more timely disclosure of policy violations, near misses and actual errors. Nonetheless, as always, reality must match the rhetoric. Organizations that implement policies, procedures and systems to encourage rapid reporting of incidents are obligated to educate their staff, evaluate changes in behavior, and then identify and resolve barriers to full compliance by making necessary refinements in their programs.

An organization that has excellent policies but does not comply with them is not only deceiving itself, it is guilty of hypocrisy and generating an illusion that will eventually harm the institution's most important stakeholders: its patients, employees, physicians, board members and the communities they serve.

Originally published in the September/October 2012 issue of *Healthcare Executive* magazine.

Discussion Questions

Describe what you believe are the top two reasons that good policies are not followed and why this is sometimes the case even in high-performing hospitals.

Why do you think some hospitals still fail to change their policies or practices after a preventable adverse event has occurred?

Trauma Care: Economic Versus Social Justice

Richard A. Culbertson, PhD

TRAUMA VIVIDLY DEMONSTRATES THE principle of the "medical commons" identified by Harvard University Dean Emeritus Howard Hiatt. The sudden and unexpected advent of the principle pushes aside traditional health disparity distinctions of economic status, race and gender in favor of proximity and skill in achieving a successful result. Trauma care and its distribution across locales provide a real-time test of the ethical perspectives identified by Peter M. Budetti, MD, JD, in his classic research as market justice versus social justice. As the provision of trauma care becomes increasingly attractive financially to providers in the current market-based model, will quality be sacrificed as a result of the inevitable reduction in the number of cases per facility?

ALL TRAUMA IS LOCAL

Traumatologists have identified the "golden hour" as highly predictive of success in trauma care. If the patient receives definitive care in the first hour following injury, chances of survival are significantly enhanced. Obviously, the patient cannot shop for trauma care, and whatever options exist in the locale of injury define the range of possibilities.

Transport to a regional facility by surface or air is typically part of an inclusive trauma system design so that injured persons receive care as rapidly as possible. States have taken a formal role in the creation of trauma system plans, which call for coordination of trauma units with lesser capabilities and transfer agreements as required to more comprehensive facilities. As of 2016, 41 states had such plans in place. In many instances, these plans impose limitations on the number of such facilities allowed to operate.

In the Indiana State Department of Health's *Trauma White Paper*, published in May 2012, the trauma system plan approach is described as "getting the right patient to the right place at the right time." The report asserts that trauma systems seek to decrease incidence of trauma and to ensure optimal, equitable and accessible care for all persons sustaining trauma. The ethical concept of justice speaks to these objectives and creates the framework for ethical analysis.

ECONOMICS OF TRAUMA CARE

Provision of high-level trauma care is costly, and cost has historically been a barrier to entry for organizations considering establishment of a comprehensive trauma facility. The American College of Surgeons crafted criteria for verification of facilities at levels of capability, ranging from the basic Level III to the full-capability Level I facility. Particular attention is paid by the ACS to availability of skilled medical personnel for Level I verification, especially the presence of an attending trauma surgeon on a 24-hour basis. A surgically directed critical care unit is mandated, as are activities related to resident training, conducting research and performing injury prevention and control.

The ACS also mandates at least 1,200 trauma patient admissions per year to maintain Level I status, which further encourages limitation of entrants into the field. As a result, most Level I facilities are major urban teaching hospitals with the ability to draw on resident physicians to buttress their capabilities. Public hospitals are particularly likely to fulfill this role as a safety-net provider with a history of tax support for trauma care that transcends hospital and physician payment from the usual public and private insurers.

Historically, trauma services were regarded as a community benefit and economic burden, the burden having caused hospitals to discontinue provision of such services. In 1990, multiple hospitals exited the Los Angeles County Trauma Network, which at that time had been considered a national model. Then-CEO of Huntington Memorial Hospital, Pasadena, California, Allen Mathies, MD, wrote in the *Los Angeles Times* that "This means that there will be some [patients] who die. The question that the public has to answer is, are deaths worse than raising taxes?"

A REVERSAL OF HISTORICAL TRENDS

More recently, the economics of trauma care have been reappraised as a result of payment changes and improvement in quality and outcomes. In urban locations, victims of penetrating trauma were often uninsured and presented a substantial financial burden to the trauma center, unless costs were offset by tax payments. With Medicaid expansion taking place in 32 states, the financial exposure for organizations has diminished, as reported in a 2017 Commonwealth Fund report. Legislation that scales back or eliminates Medicaid expansion is likely to expose safety-net hospitals to large cost increases. Motor vehicle and industrial accidents (blunt trauma) have generated predictable payment from auto insurers and workers' compensation.

Quality of care, as reflected in patient outcomes, also has improved and has been recognized favorably by the media. A 2012 Johns Hopkins/Howard University study of shootings in 2010—the most recent data available—reported improved survival rates of penetrating trauma victims, attributable in part to improved surgical techniques and postsurgical management advanced by work in the field and research by military health providers. In 2010, 13.96 percent of shooting victims died, nearly two percentage points lower than in 2007, according to the study authors.

Public support for trauma services also is high. The Indiana Department of Health reports that six in 10 Americans "would be extremely or very concerned if they found out there was no trauma center within easy reach of where they live."

INTEREST IN CREATING TRAUMA CENTERS

Although several trauma centers closed two decades ago, recent developments have demonstrated that hospitals increasingly view trauma services as desirable and feasible offerings based on community benefit and financial prospects. The University of Chicago Medicine, a private not-for-profit, has announced a major commitment to trauma services that will restore a Level I trauma center to Chicago's South Side for the first time in 25 years.

Republican Florida Governor Rick Scott has publicly stated in the *Miami Herald*, "I want to get rid of the cap on trauma centers. I want to let the private sector figure out what we should do there." His position is supported in part by a desire to see more trauma units in rural locations, in keeping with the "golden hour" principle of enhanced survival.

The expansion of trauma centers to suburban locations also has been noted in metropolitan areas such as Pittsburgh. The case mix of injuries resulting from blunt trauma has been economically more advantageous, minimizing market barriers to entry. This trend could mirror the historic pattern of dissemination of medical advances from specialty centers to community providers.

MARKET VERSUS SOCIAL JUSTICE—WHO BENEFITS?

Advocates of a market response to issues of allocative, or distributive, justice argue that the market is most efficient in achieving the ethical objective of equity in the distribution of services. Production and distribution of services are based on market demand. Social justice proponents, on the other hand, assert that healthcare is a social resource and that equitable allocation is achieved by central planning.

Broader distribution of trauma facilities would seem to benefit all under either philosophy. Yet the problem of the "commons" remains. Do new entrants diminish the quality of existing services when resources are finite? Joshua B. Brown and colleagues argue in a 2016 *Annals of Surgery* article that "Increasing volume was associated with improving outcomes, whereas decreasing volume was associated with worsening outcomes. High-level trauma center infrastructure seems to facilitate the volume-outcome relationship. The trauma center designation process should consider volume changes in the overall system."

The ethical balance here is the question of time lost in transit to a trauma facility versus dilution of highly skilled and costly services—professional and institutional—as services proliferate. An equitable and just solution to the problem of trauma care requires community-based solutions that transcend the interests of individual providers for the greatest societal benefit.

Originally published in the July/August 2017 issue of *Healthcare Executive* magazine.

Discussion Questions

The author notes that Level I trauma centers, which have more skilled physicians treating a higher volume of patients, have better clinical outcomes. In hospitals with fewer resources, what actions can executives take to facilitate the provision of timely trauma treatment to ensure distributive justice?

Centralized and well-coordinated planning is critical, but how should an executive proceed when this planning has not been effective? How can ethical principles encourage an improved planning process?

Coping with Staffing Shortages

Benn J. Greenspan, PhD, LFACHE

My organization has a range of acute clinical services that are often used to physical capacity. Because our region is experiencing broad labor shortages, staffing levels are not always what we would like or need them to be, which presents us with the dilemma of whether to continue to accept patients. What are our ethical obligations?

As it becomes increasingly difficult to fill nursing, ancillary, and other related positions, healthcare providers must be clear about the standards and objectives used to protect patients, staff, and the integrity of their organizations. While a fundamental objective of healthcare management is to ensure the well-being of patients, we must also pursue equitable, accessible, effective, and efficient provision of healthcare. Even in the best of circumstances, the simultaneous pursuit of efficacy and efficiency may require compromise between these two goals—and may also create inherent conflicts that are exacerbated when resources are limited.

In raising your question, you already recognize the conflict between the level of service you want to provide and the service that is possible with your limited resources. How can you resolve this conflict?

Triage, or rationing, is an intrinsic method of providing healthcare. Regardless of staffing levels, healthcare providers must always allocate limited resources. For example, not every patient receives one-to-one nursing care, and not every patient recovers in a bed with an automated system to minimize skin pressure. Patients are supposed to receive the care they need. When resources are limited, these decisions can be more difficult; however, it is never a question of whether we will do what is necessary, only how we will do it.

As healthcare executives, we often rely on our organizations' missions for guidance when we face such ethical dilemmas. Formulating specific guidelines in advance of staffing shortages will help your organization choose the "right" response to a real-life situation in which there is no single response—only several answers that may conflict. Taking the following actions will help you create effective policies and procedures.

Define levels of service. Openly establish a suitable understanding of what (apart from the "desired" levels of professional service) are the minimum acceptable and appropriate standard levels of service that will not compromise patient well-being. Be clear that while your organization may of course exceed the minimum acceptable standard, it must commit to never dropping below it. These levels must also be based on existing standards that have been promulgated through statute, regulation, and accreditation guidelines.

Achieve organizational consensus. Be sure that standard service levels are agreed upon with input from your staff and board. Achieving consensus through open discussion of these standards is necessary in order to

- ensure that the well-being of patients is not eclipsed by the stresses of staffing shortages,
- assure your staff that they are not being asked to offer care that is below the standards of what is expected by the profession at large,
- assure your board that your organization has exercised due process in the pursuit of standards of care,
- let all members of your community know that you are committed to optimizing your ability to deliver the best care possible, and
- satisfy your community's needs for high-quality service.

Create a reporting mechanism. Your organization must establish a mechanism through which staff can express concern when they believe that the minimum service level is being approached. As a result of using this resource, staff should expect that effective, reasonable action will be taken. The mechanism must be open, legitimate, objective, responsive, and nonretributive.

If you receive reports of subpar service, you can take one of the following actions:

- If you are a sole community provider, perform classic triage to determine who can be safely sent home.
- Shorten the length of stay for some patients. This measure can relieve resource pressure, improve organizational efficiency, and encourage alternatives—such as home care—that often improve patient satisfaction.
- Develop resource-sharing agreements with other organizations.
- In departments that are overloaded, refer patients to neighboring providers.

If the options listed are not available, you may have to take the ultimate step of refusing to provide elective patient care until the crisis period has passed. This decision might be necessary to safeguard patients, to recognize the ethical mandates of staff, and to preserve the integrity of your organization.

In following this process, we are recognizing the critical principle of nonmaleficence—attempting to minimize the potential to do harm to each patient—and its balance with the principles of beneficence and justice—alleviating the suffering of others to the broadest degree possible. By making the process open and inclusive, we are acknowledging the professional and ethical demands on our staff to pursue fidelity and honesty in serving our patients. We also maximize and benefit from the creative abilities of staff, board members, and our community in finding better ways to address important problems—a strategy that can prove invaluable in the face of an uncertain future.

Originally published in the May/June 2001 issue of *Healthcare Executive* magazine.

Discussion Questions

Acknowledging the importance of addressing the adverse consequences of staff shortages in a timely and ethical manner, how would you resolve a disagreement between employees and supervisors on whether there is an unacceptable shortage?

The author does not mention how physicians as individuals or the medical staff as an organizational body should be involved in achieving organizational consensus, so describe your strategy for engaging them in the process.

Responsibility for Unsuccessful Promotions

Paul B. Hofmann, DrPH, LFACHE

HIGHLY SKILLED CLINICAL PEOPLE are frequently promoted to management positions, but many fail to perform successfully in their new role. Is this an ethical issue? If so, how can it be avoided?

Commonly, organizations view promoting an employee as an opportunity to reward excellent work and loyalty. Although well motivated, such an action is clearly not justified if the individual is unqualified to assume supervisory responsibility. People can be attracted by more status and compensation, but if they lack management skills and interest, we unintentionally do them a great disservice by assuming everyone must want to experience the "joys" of an administrative role.

This issue is not simply an ethical matter. Nonetheless, appointing a managerially unskilled person and/or failing to deal with an incompetent supervisor can carry a very significant ethical cost. Inappropriate decisions by such an individual not only may compromise patient care but also can adversely affect subordinates, peers, and the person to whom he or she reports. Therefore, everyone is potentially compromised, including the new supervisor.

The virtues of internal promotions are important to recognize. Every progressive organization should encourage employees to pursue career advancement within their organization. Candidates for entry-level positions are usually attracted to an employer that has a strong record of internal promotions, and current staff members are more likely to remain if they witness tangible evidence of such activity. In addition, promoting an internal applicant is almost always easier, faster, and less costly than appointing someone from outside. Finally, the level of comfort and familiarity with a current employee is usually much higher in comparison with an external applicant.

PREVALENCE OF FALSE ASSUMPTIONS

Several widely held false assumptions help explain why people are often promoted beyond their level of competency.

- A person with good technical or clinical skills is qualified for a supervisory position. Because this employee is an exemplary nurse, pharmacist, physical therapist, social worker, laboratory or X-ray technologist, he or she surely will be an excellent manager.
- Every nonsupervisory employee aspires to have a management position. We have gauged our own success based upon progressing through the administrative ranks, so we believe the same is true of others.
- Individuals are unlikely to be seduced by the allure of higher pay and benefits, a new title, and perhaps an office if they are not genuinely interested in the promotion. Although these factors are important to us, the average person will be able to look objectively at the advantages and disadvantages of the new role.
- Someone invited by a supervisor, department head, or senior executive to apply for a specific opening will be entirely comfortable in declining the invitation. Despite the implicit expectation that the person will be flattered, we cannot imagine that the individual would hesitate to turn down the suggestion if there were any serious reservations.

STEPS TO PREVENT UNWISE APPOINTMENTS

Five steps are recommended to avoid the problems associated with appointing unqualified candidates:

1. Do not underestimate the leadership, planning, financial, and other skills required to perform effectively as a supervisor; make sure that the position description accurately documents the full range of responsibilities.

2. Avoid rationalizing that the time, effort, and cost of external recruitment are not worth the investment, even when viable internal candidates are available; encourage such candidates to apply to facilitate a fair comparison of qualifications.

3. Do not understate the number or magnitude of challenges inherent in the position during the interview process; a full disclosure of these challenges and the organization's expectations permits an informed decision by the successful candidate and reduces the likelihood of subsequent recriminations.

4. Identify employees who have the potential for advancement and an interest in promotional opportunities; encourage them to participate in supervisory development courses and to attend selected seminars and conferences.

5. Provide sufficient financial incentives and status to reward staff with superior skills who do not have an interest in or aptitude for significant administrative responsibility.

Almost every organization has some supervisors who are marginally capable. The managers to whom they report could be reluctant to take disciplinary action because it is personally painful and difficult. Rationalizations abound: The supervisor has been with the organization for a long time, is such a nice person, is close to retirement, is related to an influential member of the medical staff or board of trustees, is the sole income earner for the family, is likely to file a complaint, etc. An effective executive, however, who is administratively competent and ethically sensitive will take steps to minimize the number of such supervisors by creating and sustaining an organizational culture in which only truly qualified candidates are encouraged to be applicants.

Originally published in the January/February 2005 issue of *Healthcare Executive* magazine.

Discussion Questions

Some people are improperly promoted, in part because a senior manager believes they want the advantages associated with taking on more responsibility. How should a manager deal with this issue when it becomes apparent a mistake was made?

What ethically sound measures could be taken to encourage managers to make more timely decisions rather than rationalize their inaction?

Fulfilling Disruptive-Behavior Policy Objectives

Paul B. Hofmann, DrPH, LFACHE

A KEY MEMBER OF the medical staff continues to cause friction and tension in his interactions with nursing and other personnel. His behavior isn't immediately perceived as being detrimental to patient care, and the medical staff leadership is reluctant to address the situation. What ethically responsible actions should be taken?

Undeniably, disruptive behavior eventually has a negative impact on quality of care, morale and staff retention. In addition, potentially severe legal consequences may result if an organization knows or should have known about such behavior but continues to permit a hostile work environment. Almost every healthcare organization has one or more physicians who occasionally are insensitive, volatile, rude, condescending or abusive in language or behavior. Typically, such behavior is widely known and often tolerated for a variety of reasons. This person's admissions could constitute a major share of the institution's revenue; he or she could be the only physician in a critical specialty; or the individual could be politically connected with close ties to elected officials, donors or board members.

Perhaps leadership fears the individual will assert that any action taken was prejudicial and discriminatory because of his or her racial, ethnic or cultural background. If this fear exists, possible litigation is a legitimate concern, particularly if a physician's privileges are suspended. Similarly, if a physician has chronically complained about perceived deficiencies in quality of care and personnel shortcomings prior to becoming the subject of a disruptive-behavior investigation, it is likely the physician will allege the investigation is an act of retaliation.

In such situations, denying or rationalizing inappropriate behavior is common. We are told, "The problem is really not that severe." We also hear, "Actually, it is just the result of some people being overly sensitive" or "The timing isn't right" or "The physician is close to retirement, so everything will be resolved without the need for any formal intervention."

NO EASY SOLUTIONS

So-called experts who suggest that applying a standard disruptive-behavior policy is simple or straightforward probably have not had much personal experience in doing it themselves. It is almost impossible to avoid some degree of anxiety and stress in such a situation, which usually affects all the stakeholders.

However, when staff members are intimidated by physicians who exhibit threatening behavior, a severe impact on both patient care and staff morale is unavoidable. For instance, innumerable surveys and studies have confirmed that nurses and other caregivers are much less likely to question or request clarification of a physician's order if they fear being verbally abused.

The following steps to apply a disruptive-behavior policy should be self-evident, but familiarity is not sufficient—they must be taken promptly when circumstances require timely intervention.

1. Ensure that all members of the medical staff are aware of existing policies and procedures pertaining to disruptive behavior. These policies and procedures should be comprehensive: identifying their purpose; defining terms (such as *discriminatory behavior, harassment* and *disruptive behavior*); providing reporting guidelines; establishing time requirements; outlining options depending on

the outcome of investigations; prohibiting retaliation against complainants; noting actions to be taken if false complaints are submitted; and describing the responsibilities of medical staff officers and committees, senior executives and the governing body.

2. Comply with these policies and procedures when initiating the process.
3. Collaborate closely with the medical staff leadership.
4. Consult with the organization's legal counsel.
5. Conduct all inquiries and meetings in a confidential and respectful manner.
6. Provide ample opportunity to allow the physician to respond to all allegations.
7. Document both informal and formal meetings.
8. Keep the governing body's leaders informed.

Clearly, it is insufficient to focus exclusively on addressing problems once they have occurred. Effective leaders are those who recognize their inherent responsibility to create and sustain an organizational culture that promotes collegial relationships and has zero tolerance for inappropriate conduct. By modeling proper behavior, leaders demonstrate they are truly committed to building and sustaining a culture of genuine teamwork and collaboration.

While a wide variety of actions have been taken by progressive institutions to maintain a supportive, productive and professionally satisfying working environment, the most basic elements include:

- Providing educational and training programs concerning this sensitive topic
- Performing periodic surveys of staff members regarding their satisfaction with their working environment
- Monitoring compliance with codes of conduct and disruptive-behavior policies

- Having simple and convenient means for reporting concerns
- Investigating all allegations promptly and thoroughly
- Giving timely feedback on all complaints submitted
- Making anger management and similar support services available under the auspices of a physician well-being committee and employee assistance program

CEOs and governing boards have a key role to play in monitoring an organization's culture, especially its influence on safety and quality. John Combes, MD, president and chief operating officer of the American Hospital Association's Center for Healthcare Governance, has noted that an excellent culture is difficult to create but easy to break. By allowing disruptive behavior, he says, all the hard work that went into creating a culture of reliability and quality can be instantly destroyed.

FINAL OBSERVATIONS

An increasing number of helpful publications are now available on this topic. For example, "Disruptive Physicians" is an excellent article by Karen Sandrick in the November/December 2009 issue of *Trustee* magazine. She reminds readers that The Joint Commission's July 2008 *Sentinel Event Alert* warned hospitals that "disruptive behavior can lead to medical errors, erode patient satisfaction, play a part in causing preventable adverse outcomes, raise the cost of patient care, and increase clinician and staff turnover."

In the November/December 2009 issue of *Physician Executive Journal*, Carrie Johnson authored "Bad Blood: Doctor–Nurse Behavior Problems Impact Patient Care," summarizing the disturbing results of an electronic survey sent to approximately 13,000 physicians and nurses. Also recommended is *A Practical Guide to Preventing and Solving Disruptive Physician Behavior*, a superb book coauthored by Richard Sheff, MD, and Todd Sagin, MD, JD (HCPro, 2004).

Executives must not abdicate their responsibility to take seriously any allegation of disruptive behavior. Productive collaboration and quality improvement are inhibited or impossible to achieve when disruptive behavior is permitted. Although this discussion has focused on physicians, certainly the problem of disruptive behavior is not limited to them. This reality is recognized by The Joint Commission's latest leadership standards dealing with conflict management and maintaining a culture of safety.

Ultimately, regardless of external mandates, effective organizational leaders realize the toughest ethical and behavioral problems will only become exacerbated through inattention. The stakes are much too high not to deal forthrightly with intimidation and other unprofessional conduct. Because abusive attitudes, language and behavior have no place in our healing institutions, it is morally imperative to move quickly and effectively.

Originally published in the May/June 2010 issue of *Healthcare Executive* magazine.

Discussion Questions

When staff members and management permit disruptive behavior by physicians or others in influential positions, what additional steps might be taken beyond those recommended by the author?

Suggest two or three questions that should be included in a staff satisfaction survey to determine whether this issue is a prevalent concern.

---

7 Factors Complicate Ethical Resource Allocation Decisions

Paul B. Hofmann, DrPH, LFACHE

SERIOUS CHALLENGES ARE ENDEMIC in complex healthcare organizations. To address them effectively, regardless of the situation, we first must be conscious of the ethical dimensions and implications of our decisions as well as our behavior.

Continuing financial constraints indicate the need to devote special attention to specific factors that increase the ethical challenges that accompany resource allocation decisions. The provision of optimal patient care will increasingly depend on our ability to face these challenges successfully.

ILLUSTRATIVE CASE

The chief of radiology reports that an impressive new technology is now available that will significantly improve diagnostic accuracy in assessing malignant tumors. Although it is expensive, oncologists are insisting its acquisition is essential to properly evaluate patients and to remain competitive with other hospitals that have placed orders for this equipment. But you have already received equally compelling requests from other key clinical leaders in cardiac surgery and obstetrics. In addition, you are painfully aware that, to accommodate comparable needs in the past, you have delayed replacing the hospital's roof and upgrading one of the intensive care units for the last three years. And, of course, expanding the new electronic medical record system is running substantially above budget.

Predictably, the hospital does not have sufficient funds to meet all these demands. Complicating the situation, the chief of radiology's father is on the hospital's board of directors, and he has made it clear that you are expected to approve the diagnostic equipment request. And the chief of cardiac surgery has been describing how new robotic surgery equipment might be funded by one of his wealthy friends. The obstetrical chief has said the area designated for expansion of the OB unit must be completed now to accommodate the higher number of deliveries. Unfortunately, you believe the cost and revenue estimates for some of these projects are questionable, but you lack sufficient time to obtain a more complete cost/benefit analysis.

This case illustrates the seven most common issues encountered in making difficult resource allocation decisions, each with a distinct ethical component:

1. Inadequate funds to support equally compelling requests
2. Strong opinions expressed by influential and politically powerful people
3. Severe time constraints, making it difficult to conduct comprehensive and objective analyses of multiple variables
4. Significant conflicts of interest
5. Uncertainty about potential outcomes and unintentional consequences
6. Competing professional and personal values
7. The possibility that the decision could have a negative impact on job security

Everyone agrees that the number of requests for capital projects will continue to exceed available resources in the foreseeable future. Undeniably, one or more of the above issues will consciously or unconsciously affect the decision-making process. So the ethical challenge is to determine how these conflicts and dilemmas can be properly addressed.

ETHICAL GUIDELINES

The guidelines for making sound resource allocation decisions from an ethical perspective are similar to those that should be followed for most executive decisions. The key points include transparency, honesty, integrity, promise-keeping, stewardship, fairness and alignment with the organization's vision, mission and values.

The ability to address many of these points depends on:

- accepting accountability
- maintaining credibility
- fulfilling past commitments
- demonstrating objectivity
- showing respect for legitimate differences of opinion
- distinguishing between rhetoric and reality
- acquiring reliable and comprehensive information
- recognizing the inability to satisfy all proponents despite the validity of their requests
- developing a defensible rationale for the decision
- obtaining support from key stakeholders
- communicating effectively

The illustrative case provides an opportunity to test the utility and practicality of applying both personal and professional ethical guidelines. As suggested in a previous column ("Allocating Limited Capital Resources," *Healthcare Executive*, March/April 2000), the ethical principles of beneficence, nonmaleficence, fidelity and justice should also be considered in making a sound decision. When presented with an ethical dilemma, five questions can help frame the evaluation process:

1. What are the relevant ethical facts?
2. What additional information is needed?
3. What are the specific ethical questions or value conflicts?
4. How would you respond to them?
5. What is the ethical basis for your thinking?

The answers to these questions will not automatically produce the ideal solution, but in combination with the points emphasized above, they will increase the probability of a defensible decision, particularly when answered in consultation with others.

Making tough choices intelligently and ethically must be every executive's highest priority. Competent subordinates are expected to make the easier decisions. Eventually, with consistent mentoring and by learning from their mistakes, they, too, will be better prepared to weigh competing values and to choose wisely among them, helping to ensure continuity in ethical decision making throughout the organization and into the future. Although there is no comprehensive ethical cookbook with unambiguous recipes for every potential dilemma, progressive leaders anticipate unavoidable ethical dilemmas and think creatively about how to approach them.

Genuine ethical dilemmas do not always have a "right" answer. Reasonable people can argue passionately for different positions without compromising an organization's formally adopted ethical criteria. Competent management relies extensively on relationships based on authority, power, trust and integrity. To a large degree, ethical behavior is about each of these and the obligation of executives not to abuse or corrupt them.

Originally published in the May/June 2011 issue of *Healthcare Executive* magazine.

Discussion Questions

Given that requests for increased capital expenditures will exceed available resources, how would you ensure the validity of each proposal's cost-effectiveness projections?

The availability of limited funds means proponents of unapproved proposals will be disappointed. Suggest a few constructive recommendations for handling this challenge.

Ethics: A Foundation for Quality

William A. Nelson, PhD, HFACHE

A QUESTION RARELY, IF ever, raised in executive ethics training is, "Is ethics important for healthcare organizations?" The participants' presence suggests an interest in and commitment to the importance of ethics.

But while no executive would ever indicate that ethical values are unimportant, do executives regularly acknowledge, demonstrate and ensure ethical values are the foundation and framework for today's healthcare organizations? If staff were surveyed, would they report that ethical values serve as the organization's foundation and framework?

ETHICAL VALUES AS THE ORGANIZATION'S FOUNDATION

Basic ethics principles that make up our common morality, including respect for patients, acting in patients' best interest, avoiding bringing harm to patients and treating patients in a fair and equitable manner, serve as the foundation for healthcare values. These values are generally captured in the organization's mission and values statements.

In thinking about the importance of values as the organization's foundation, consider the construction of a home. After the building site is cleared and the concrete forms have been placed, the cement is poured, creating the concrete foundation. The foundation becomes the base that will support the load of the structure; its contents and all that occurs within it will rest on that foundation. Similarly, achieving a healthcare organization's purpose depends on having a strong foundation. But rather than a concrete foundation, the hospital or health system's foundation is its ethics.

ETHICAL VALUES AS THE ORGANIZATION'S FRAMEWORK

Ethical values also serve as the organization's framework. In a building, the framework gives shape to the various activities and functions within the structure. Analogously, ethical values frame the guidelines for the organization's operations. They guide staff in how to "live out" that foundation in its overall culture and administrative and clinical practices, which ultimately affects patient encounters.

The culture should reflect organizational values in the behaviors of all individual staff members and in organizationwide actions. For example, clinical practices should consistently reflect organizational values such as promoting patient self-determination in end-of-life decision making. Management decisions should be based on and reflect the organization's values as well, such as in crafting physician compensation guidelines in a manner that avoids conflicts of interest.

Applying ethical values as the foundation and framework for today's healthcare organizations can be particularly challenging because of economic tensions so common in the delivery of care. For example, do you purchase a new CT scanner because it will generate a larger revenue stream or because evidence supports the belief that the scanner will improve patient care? Which is the real, underlying rationale for the potential purchase? Does it correlate with the organization's values? Professor Kurt Darr, in *Ethics in Health Services Management* (Health Professions Press, 2004), reminds executives that when considering such a purchase, "Health service organizations are social enterprises with an economic dimension rather than an economic enterprise with a social dimension."

When ethics challenges arise in either the clinical or administrative setting, ethical reasoning can serve as a useful tool in addressing the conflict, highlighting a second role of ethical values in the organization's framework. Regarding the example of resource allocation noted earlier, healthcare executives need to recognize that such decisions raise ethical questions and must be considered within the context of the organization's values.

Ethics resources, such as an ethics committee member or a healthcare ethicist who can effectively facilitate ethics reflection, need to be available and should have a seat at the table when such decisions are being made. The process can decrease the presence of an organization's values–practice gap and ensure organizational values serve as the foundation and framework—not just words on some document.

THE ETHICS, QUALITY AND VALUE LINKAGE

Recognizing ethical values as the foundation and framework for healthcare organizations is directly tied to the quest for quality and value in the delivery of care. The pursuit of quality and value is based on the application of ethics principles and values, including autonomy, beneficence, nonmaleficence, and social and distributive justice. These basic ethics principles are the foundation for the Institute of Medicine's (IoM) six aims for improving healthcare, as proposed in its landmark report *Crossing the Quality Chasm* (National Academies Press, 2001): patient-centered, effective, safe, efficient, timely and equitable.

Ethics values provide the underlying reasons that quality aims and economic value are essential for healthcare organizations. The same ethics values that serve as the foundation and framework for healthcare serve as the basis of quality goals. When facilities seek to fulfill the IoM's six quality aims, they are also seeking to provide ethics-grounded healthcare. The chart below (adapted from "Preventing Ethics Conflicts and Improving Healthcare Quality," Nelson and colleagues, *Quality and Safety in Health Care*, 2010) highlights the linkage between ethical values, quality and economic value.

Ethics Principles	Applications of Ethics Values to Quality Care	IOM's Quality Aims
Autonomy	Support, facilitate and respect patient self-determination; promote the consistent application of a shared decision-making process	Patient-centered
Beneficence	Ensure beneficial patient healthcare is uniformly implemented; make certain the patient's best interest is paramount	Effective, safe, timely, patient-centered
Nonmaleficence	Avoid and protect the patient from actions that cause harm	Safe, effective, patient-centered
Social and distributive justice	Provide fair allocation of resources to support the patient's best interest, impartial distribution of the benefits and burdens related to delivery of healthcare, and equitable access to healthcare services	Equitable, efficient, patient-centered

The connection between quality and ethics becomes apparent when ethics conflicts occur or quality issues arise. When organizational quality is compromised, ethics norms or standards of practice are frequently violated or eroded. For example, when healthcare professionals provide nonbeneficial or futile care, they erode the organization's quality aims of providing only effective, patient-centered care, which correspond to the ethical norms of providing only beneficial patient care and avoiding actions that can cause harm. Additionally, in such situations, physician decisions can waste organization or third-party economic resources because the margin of benefit per unit of expenditure lacks value.

Similarly, when ethics issues occur, quality aims and care can be compromised. For example, when healthcare professionals willfully ignore patient decisions or do not provide full, open and truthful information regarding an invasive procedure to a terminally ill patient, or when they fail to disclose an adverse event, the quality standard of patient-centered care is not met, nor is the ethical standard of respecting self-determination. In these examples you can see that synergy between ethics, quality and value reinforces the need for executives to recognize the importance of ethical values to healthcare organizations.

CHARACTERISTICS OF ORGANIZATIONS WITH AN ETHICS-GROUNDED FOUNDATION AND FRAMEWORK

Several general characteristics in healthcare organizations reflect the recognition of ethical values serving as the organization's foundation and framework.

Ethical leadership—The organization's leadership acknowledges and consistently demonstrates the importance of ethics in his or her decisions and actions. Leadership expects that managers and supervisors serve as ethics role models to the staff they are directing. Leaders support and use ethics resources and mechanisms.

Integrated mission and ethical values—The mission and ethical values are clearly understood by all staff and serve as the driver for the organization's actions.

Ethics culture and practice—The organizational values are recognized and integrated into the daily actions and behavior of all staff. The values provide identity to the staff and the organization and are consistently embodied in all clinical and administrative practices.

Effective ethics programs linked with the quality program—The organization has an effective ethics program that is comprehensive, staff and leadership supported and respected, and that addresses administrative and clinical ethics issues in a system-oriented, reactive and proactive manner. Rather than operating in a silo, the program is linked to quality improvement, patient safety and compliance to ultimately foster and ensure quality patient care. Healthcare leaders need to be serious about the importance of ethics to their organizations—it is not just window dressing. Ensuring that your organization has an ethics-grounded foundation and framework can be a primary factor in determining whether your organization successfully provides value and quality of care to the community it serves.

Originally published in the November/December 2011 issue of *Healthcare Executive* magazine.

Discussion Questions

The author presents the concept that ethics are foundational to an organization's quest for value and quality in patient care. What basic ethical principles support the focus on value and quality?

How does the quote from Kurt Darr ("Health service organizations are social enterprises with an economic dimension rather than an economic enterprise with a social dimension") relate to the healthcare organization with which you are most familiar?

Ethics and Advertising

William A. Nelson, PhD, HFACHE, and Emily C. Taylor

As HOSPITALS AND OTHER healthcare facilities struggle to attract and retain patients, they frequently engage in advertising campaigns. This form of communication can be extremely effective in achieving the goals of increasing revenue and market share. Although extensive discussions have taken place regarding the content of consumer-directed advertisements by pharmaceutical companies, advertisements by hospitals have received little attention despite the increased use of consumer-directed methods.

We believe hospitals and other healthcare facilities must be ethically grounded in their messaging and ensure that what they communicate in advertisements, like any other action, reflects their organization's mission, vision and values. To this end, healthcare executives should consider developing ethics guidelines, including a review process, for their advertising efforts.

Advertising can be defined as any activity aimed at calling attention to one's products or services, with the goal of increasing consumption. Hospital advertising can be indirect, such as highlighting recent successes, awards or low costs to improve name recognition or awareness of general advantages over competitors. It can also be direct, such as promoting specific services, treatments or procedures. The growing phenomenon of advertising in the healthcare industry increasingly does the latter, targeting specific messages about specific services to specific populations.

Although the ultimate goal of these advertising approaches may be the same—to attract customers—the methods often differ in ways that raise various ethical issues.

Because medical interventions can inherently carry a degree of risk, and advertisements for these interventions can lack proper disclosure of those risks, potential consumers of these services are generally considered to be vulnerable. For that reason, the U.S. Food and Drug Administration reviews certain types of direct-to-consumer advertisements by pharmaceutical companies to help reconcile the safety of the potential patient with the commercial goal of the advertisement.

Presently, however, no governmental body exists to review direct-to-consumer advertisements by hospitals or physicians targeting a similar audience. The Federal Trade Commission Act prohibits "unfair or deceptive acts or practices in or affecting commerce," but without an external review process in place, organizations are left alone to determine the goal and potential outcomes of an advertisement.

It appears that few healthcare facilities use formal mechanisms to review the appropriateness of direct-to-consumer advertisements. A 2005 study by Robin Larson, MD, et al., which appeared in the *Archives of Internal Medicine*, examined print advertisements by academic medical centers, noting that most advertising fits into one of three categories: (1) raising general name recognition; (2) increasing awareness of specific departments or bundled offerings (spine center, cancer center, etc.); or (3) promoting discrete services.

The study found that the most commonly used marketing strategies "capitalize on emotional appeals, institution prestige, self-diagnosis, and gateway offers," and many advertisements for discrete services promote unproven or cosmetic procedures and screenings. The study also revealed that only one of the 17 top academic medical centers surveyed had a formal review process for advertisements to attract patients. This is in contrast to advertisements aimed at recruiting research study participants, which must undergo formal review by the hospital's institutional review board.

Without formal processes in place for reviewing hospital advertisements aimed at attracting patients, no mechanism exists to ensure that the information conveyed in these messages is sound and ethically grounded. Hospital executives must lead their organizations in creating a culture for responsible advertising. They should ensure their marketing departments have a set of guidelines for advertising that guarantees all advertisements are in line with the organization's patient-centered mission, vision and values. If a hospital's mission, vision and values are aligned to promote safe, quality, effective, efficient and value-driven care for its patients, then all communications, including advertisements, should be a means to that end.

DEVELOPING A FORMAL REVIEW PROCESS

Any advertising effort should be reviewed using a standardized approach. The process of creating and reviewing the advertisement should be the responsibility of the marketing department in close collaboration with the organization's leadership and ethics committees. The overall goal of a review is to ensure there is alignment between an advertisement and the organization's mission and values. For example, an advertisement by a healthcare organization that contains statements that are false, lack scientific evidence or are misleading, including statements that mislead by purposely omitting necessary information, should be considered unethical.

The process for achieving a systematic review of an advertisement may begin with the director of marketing initially reviewing an advertisement, followed by clinicians or appropriate professionals knowledgeable about the topic and an "outside" reviewer, such as a community representative, to diminish any potential conflict of interest. This process is similar to that used by institutional review boards and ethics committees.

If there is disagreement, concern or uncertainty about the ethical integrity of the messaging, the director of marketing should call upon the ethics committee for consultation. The organization's leadership should support this process by offering clear mission, vision and values statements with which the marketing department can align its communications.

Below is a set of basic questions that can assist marketing departments when designing or reviewing an advertisement to ensure that the communication is ethically grounded, while still being effective.

When reviewing a particular advertisement, the marketing department should consider:

- **The purpose of the advertisement.** Advertisements should have a statement of purpose that can be clearly articulated during the review process. The statement of purpose should consider the target audience and align with the organization's patient-centered mission, vision and values. To help determine the statement of purpose, the following questions can be asked: What is the goal of this advertisement? What is the advertisement saying and to whom? What are possible unforeseen consequences of the advertisement? Does the advertisement balance the organization's desire to increase market share with the goal of improving the community's health?

- **The choice of language and images.** Advertisements should be ethically grounded in their communication, both in language and images. Advertisements should use language that can be supported by facts and is balanced, clear, concise, honest, accurate and responsible. Images should support the language in conveying the intended message. Neither the language nor the choice of images should be deceptive or misleading or cause people to gain a false sense of trust in the organization or an exaggerated sense of the value of a specific service being promoted. The language and images should convey a message that is responsible, supports the advertisement's intended purpose and is in line with the organization's mission, vision and values.

- **Possible outcomes of the advertisement.** A protocol should be in place to evaluate whether the intended purpose of the advertisement is being accomplished or if another outcome has resulted. A standard of appropriate effectiveness should exist.

Adhering to the above review process will guide a hospital's marketing department to act ethically when designing and reviewing advertisements. The dual goals of hospital advertisements should be to increase revenue and market share, and to act in the best interest of a potential patient.

Following a review process to balance these goals will assist the organization in acting ethically and avoiding a potential conflict of interest. In addition, it will ensure the hospital communicates a consistent message across all its platforms and through all its actions. Advertising is an important form of communication for any organization looking to balance its desire to increase revenue and market share in concert with its commitment to the organization's values and to the community's well-being. But, without a formal external review process in place for hospital advertising, it is the responsibility of the hospital to review its communications internally. This will no doubt earn the organization a heightened reputation in the community and contribute to organizational success.

Originally published in the March/April 2012 issue of *Healthcare Executive* magazine.

Discussion Questions

Describe the basic ethical concepts that should be fundamental to healthcare advertising.

The author argues that a formal review process should be employed to assess the ethical integrity of advertisements. Of the three steps recommended, which two do you think are most important and why?

Comparing Ethics and Compliance Programs

William A. Nelson, PhD, HFACHE

RECENTLY I WAS SPEAKING at a healthcare management training program and made the brief comment that ethics and compliance programs overlap in their focus, yet are not the same. During the question and answer period I was pushed to clarify the distinction, which I attempted to do. Following the training session, a respected hospital CEO approached me and noted that the distinction I had suggested was new to him. I was somewhat surprised by his comment, but as I have reflected on the difference between compliance and ethics programs following our exchange, I sense his sentiment is not unique.

The early Renaissance poet Dante Alighieri helps to clarify the difference between ethics and compliance in a famous letter to his benefactor, Can Grande. The letter details how Dante's epic poem "The Divine Comedy" can be interpreted. In the letter, Dante indicates that the poem can be understood on four levels: the *literal* level or the basic story; the *allegorical* level, focusing on the myths and heroes of the poem; the *moral* or *compliance* level, highlighting what society expects of us through law and custom; and, finally, the deepest level—the *ethics* level—emphasizing how we can be nurtured by principles, values and humanism. Dante's distinction between compliance and ethics is a useful starting point for today's healthcare organizations to think about this topic.

ETHICS VS. COMPLIANCE PROGRAMS

The definition of "compliance" refers to an act or a process of complying with a demand or conforming to official requirements. As Dante's description of "The Divine Comedy" suggests, compliance refers to societal expectations of obedience to laws and regulations. In healthcare organizations, compliance programs inform and monitor adherence to specific state and federal laws and regulations and third-party guidelines by designing and implementing internal controls, policies and procedures. Compliance programs inform and monitor organizations regarding such activities as billing, coding, reimbursements and potential conflicts of interest. These programs also manage audits and investigations into regulatory and compliance issues and respond to requests for information from regulatory bodies.

Compliance with regulatory mandates is a critical component of effective risk management, enabling an organization to better prevent, discover and respond to violations in a way that is in alignment with societal expectations. Compliant behavior works to reduce the risk of costly litigation, bad press and the loss of community support of a healthcare organization.

Being compliant with laws and regulations is one expression of the shared values of a community or society. Richard E. Cohan, FACHE, pointed out in a *Healthcare Management* Ethics column in the January/February 2004 issue of *Healthcare Executive* that compliant behavior means that staff obeys the laws and regulations that must be followed "to operate your healthcare business in the context of healthcare businesses in your state and/or across the country."

The law, and the compliance programs that ensure organizations abide by it, establishes minimally acceptable standards of conduct and rarely provides conclusive guidance when ethics conflicts occur. Cohan further suggested that compared to compliance, ethics "takes an organization to the next level—a level at which decisions are made not only to comply with the law, but furthermore, to always do the right thing." In other words, organizational actions and decisions must consistently correlate with societal, organizational and professional values—not only the law.

Forming the foundation of ethics programs are our common values (respect, integrity, etc.); ethics principles, such as acting in the patient's interest, promoting patient autonomy and avoiding harm; and profession-focused codes of ethics. Ethics programs provide organizations with a set of fundamental values that are reflected in values and mission statements.

Whereas compliance focuses on risk management, ethics programs seek to ensure the delivery of high-quality, safe and patient-centered healthcare through the integration of common values into the organization's overall culture, including in all staff members' actions.

Ethics programs are also designed to clarify uncertainty or resolve conflicts related to shared values. Ethics consultation, a key component of many ethics programs, provides case consultations to address ethics questions related to competing values. For example, when an autonomous patient insists on a treatment that a physician believes, based on scientific evidence, is medically inappropriate, an ethics consultation team may be brought in to help address the competing values of the patient and the physician.

Ethics program members are trained to handle conflicts and the related questions that arise between ethics principles through systematic ethical reasoning. Whether the physician is morally obligated to provide nonbeneficial care is not a question the compliance program is equipped to answer, as this issue does not relate to the law. The issue relates to addressing or possibly ranking the competing values and deciding who the moral agent is in decision making when there are various involved stakeholders.

OVERLAP BETWEEN ETHICS AND COMPLIANCE PROGRAMS

Despite the distinction between them, ethics and compliance programs overlap in several ways. Both seek to foster the fulfillment of a healthcare organization's mission and values, but their foundations and approaches to this goal are unique.

The overlap relates to the relationship between ethics and law. As the late philosopher Bernard Gert described in his book *Common Morality: Deciding What to Do* (Oxford University Press, 2004), one of society's common guiding moral rules is the duty to obey the law.

Situations arise, however, when adherence to the law gives rise to an ethical question. For example, when an individual is driving down a road and approaches a stop sign, he or she is expected to stop in compliance with the law. When that individual respects the law, society's common value of acting in a way that diminishes and avoids harm is promoted. On the other hand, if that same individual drives on that same road in an emergency situation, rushing to get an injured passenger to an emergency room, would he or she be required to stop?

This situation highlights an ethical conflict due to competing values: obeying the law versus promoting the injured passenger's well-being. The ethics question in this situation would be: Is the individual morally justified in disregarding the stop sign (or at least proceeding through it cautiously) in the attempt to rescue the injured passenger? Being compliant with the law and acting in the best interest of another human being are unique in this situation, highlighting the sometimes-complex overlap of compliance and ethics.

Because adherence to and compliance with the law are part of our common morality—and because our common morality is what ethics programs aim to uphold—the two programs do overlap. As a result, it is the shared responsibility of the compliance officer and the ethics consultant to be aware of the differences between these programs and their missions, to reflect upon this difference and to seek one another's assistance when overlap exists. In a practice approach, these two programs should be unique, but members of a compliance office should be active participants of ethics programs and vice versa.

Originally published in the July/August 2012 issue of *Healthcare Executive* magazine.

Discussion Questions

The author indicates that compliance and ethics programs overlap but are different. How would you describe the distinction between the two important programs?

Explain how the ethics and compliance programs might collaborate in an organization.

A Reflection on Everyday Ethics

Jack A. Gilbert, EdD

AT THE END OF the day, doing the right thing does not depend on the quality of compliance programs, ethics training, hotlines and the like, although they are valuable. When the Ethics Resource Center, a nonprofit, nonpartisan research organization, looked over results from its cross-industry 2011 National Business Ethics Survey spanning more than 10 years, it concluded that ethics programs had not produced the expected positive results and that *organizational culture* was more influential in strengthening ethical behavior.

I suggest that an ethical organizational culture depends on the choices leaders, and indeed every person in the organization, make in those small, often unexpected moments when our values rub up against reality. No matter what our position in the organization, what each of us does or does not do, says or does not say, these moments determine how well we as leaders and our organizations meet the enduring challenge of doing the right thing and being true to our organizations' vision, mission and values.

These are not easy moments. Speaking up can take all the courage we can muster when we feel that speaking up is a risk for any number of reasons, including not wanting to provoke a confrontation, wanting to be a team player by going along with a course of action even if we disagree, deferral to authority and not wanting to waste others' time in a meeting. Even so, they are important moments personally as well as professionally because part of what is at stake is our personal integrity; that wholeness and peace we experience when our own goals, actions and decisions are consistent with our most cherished values.

I ask you to consider that the degree to which we nurture our personal integrity hinges on three daily disciplines that when practiced can lead us to continually strengthen not only our personal integrity but our organization's ethical culture. Those daily disciplines are personal legacy, mindfulness and voice.

PERSONAL LEGACY

Personal legacy is what we build for others during and after our lives through our work and our relationships. It is the highest expression of our goals and aspirations. The dictionary defines legacy as "a gift" and "something handed down by a predecessor." As a daily practice it is clarity about our "true north," the guiding light of our lives.

Why is this so important? Consider the alternative expressed through the proverb, "If you don't know where you are going, any direction will do." If what we stand for is not front and center when the pressure is intense (as it often is in the life of a leader), we are more likely to act from expediency than from our personal legacy and our values, with all the negative consequences that arise as others look to our example as a guide to their own decision making.

Take some time to reflect on your personal legacy, your life purpose, by yourself or in conversation with those close to you. Express it in a few words you can easily remember and remind yourself of it every day, most simply by putting it in your daily calendar. Do not doubt that your life is significant. In the words of Mother Teresa, "We ourselves feel that what we are doing is just a drop in the ocean. But the ocean would be less because of that missing drop."

You already do things every day that are a gift to others. Notice them more. Acknowledge them more, in yourself and others. Be even more purposeful about focusing on what matters most to you.

Then leverage this focus on your personal legacy to strengthen your organization's legacy found in its vision, mission and values. Like our personal legacy it easily falls silent, drowned out by the everyday noise. The same principles of personal legacy apply: create daily or weekly opportunities for your team to recommit to the vision, mission and values—not with rhetorical commitment (e.g., words without action), but with words matched by action as team members find ways to enliven the vision, mission and values with their own employees and use them as an everyday framework for decision making. This is what CEO Gary S. Kaplan, MD, FACP, FACMPE, FACPE, has sought to create at Virginia Mason Health System through decision making that is seen through a hierarchy of patient, organization, department and individual, in that order.

MINDFULNESS

This leads us to the second daily discipline, *mindfulness,* which in this context means being alert to personal and organizational integrity as we move through a busy and distracting day. When asked about truth, Mahatma Gandhi once responded, "What is truth? A difficult question; but I have solved it for myself by saying that it is what the 'voice within' tells you."

All well and good, but how do we know our "voice within?" We know it by being sensitive to how it "speaks" to us. It most often takes the form of a faint signal expressed as an emotional or physical reaction. It might be a sense of calm or comfort with the direction of a conversation or decision. Or it might be the opposite, a sense of unease. It might be a gut reaction, a physical discomfort or a nagging doubt that something is "off" with a decision. Or it might be the opposite, a sense of physical relaxation. These are sometimes called faint signals, and they are worth attending to as a register for whether a decision is resonant or dissonant with our personal integrity—our sense of wholeness and peace. In the organizational context these faint signals indicate consistency with the organization's "true north."

As a daily discipline, being mindful is challenging. It is so easy to push aside or shut off our connection to our emotions and to our physical reactions. But these faint signals, different from our biases and assumptions, are clues to the health of our personal integrity and by extension to the organization's integrity. A simple reminder in front of you during conversations and meetings may suffice to raise your self-awareness, such as a note that asks, "What am I feeling about this right now?"

VOICE

If mindfulness is the inner expression of ethical wisdom then *voice*, the third daily discipline, is the public expression. It brings mindfulness into open conversation, enabling ethical issues to be revealed and explored in a constructive spirit in meetings, informal conversations and everyday work. There are two aspects to voice. First, the choice we make to claim our own voice, usually easier for executives than for those lower in the organization. And second, the opportunity to share voice that is provided to everyone in everyday work exchanges.

Viktor Frankl, psychiatrist and famous World War II concentration camp survivor, when writing about life and death in the most extreme of human circumstances, said, "What matters . . . is not the meaning of life in general but rather the specific meaning of a person's life at a given moment." There are many moments, no matter what our place in the organization, when we are challenged to stand up for our values or for the organization's values. Sometimes we make decisions that disappoint us; sometimes we make decisions that evoke pride. We are all susceptible to falling short—to having our personal integrity fly out the window under the pressures we face to make snap decisions, or decisions under threat from others or from within ourselves.

Given all this, organizational encouragement to claim our voice and to speak up in these difficult moments is essential to our personal integrity and equally essential to the ethical health of the organization. The 2011 National Business Ethics Survey, which includes healthcare organizations, reported that 45 percent of employees surveyed observed at least one instance of ethical misconduct at work in the past year and that 35 percent of those employees did not report the violation to management. Of those who did report, 22 percent experienced some form of retaliation. So giving voice to all employees is a critical issue.

Do you allow any time when a decision is being made for someone to be able to express his or her discomfort with the direction of a decision? Are your meetings so fast paced, so packed with agenda items, that they impede the expression of discomfort because no one wants to be accused of slowing the meeting or of not being a team player by expressing doubts? Do employees tell you that they are comfortable bringing unethical acts to light? If your answer as a senior leader is "no" or "I don't know" to these questions, then I can assure you the majority of meetings (and many other encounters) in your organization will reflect the precedent you are setting and that honest sharing of ethical issues or doubts is pervasively discouraged.

Let me again acknowledge that while the daily disciplines of being clear on our personal legacy, being mindful of the faint signals that put us in touch with our own wisdom, and claiming and allowing voice are challenging, their consistent practice is worthwhile because of the contribution to our own sense of well-being and our organizations' ethical health.

Magda Trocme was a hero of World War II who participated in saving many Jewish children under dangerous circumstances. I think the lessons she drew from her experience are important to us today. After the war, Trocme said of her experiences, "Remember that in your life there will be lots of circumstances that will need a kind of courage, a kind of decision of your own, not about other people but about yourself."

Originally published in the January/February 2013 issue of *Healthcare Executive* magazine.

Discussion Questions

The author encourages us to describe our personal legacy (our life purpose) in a few words easily remembered. What do you hope will be your legacy?

Offer some insights about how to (a) remain mindful under difficult circumstances and (b) find ways to publicly express concerns that if unspoken would be to the detriment of the organization and your personal integrity.

The Ethics of Mandatory Flu Shots

William A. Nelson, PhD, HFACHE,
and Tim Lahey, MD

INFLUENZA IS A COMMON, life-threatening and vaccine-preventable infection. The transmission of influenza in hospitals and other healthcare facilities is a major safety issue, particularly for hospitalized patients.

Influenza vaccination is effective at preventing the spread of influenza, so the U.S. Advisory Committee on Immunization Practices recommends influenza immunization for everyone older than 6 months. More specifically, according to a February 2011 article in the *American Journal of Public Health* by Abigale L. Ottenberg et al., influenza immunization of healthcare workers is recommended to 1) prevent transmission to patients; 2) reduce the risk of healthcare workers becoming infected; 3) maintain a societal workforce of healthcare workers; and 4) create an example of the need and importance of vaccination.

Despite the clear indications for influenza immunization among healthcare workers, a 2010 position paper authored by Thomas Talbot, MD, et al., for the Society for Healthcare Epidemiology of America, notes that "despite tremendous efforts to promote HCP [healthcare personnel] influenza vaccinations by government agencies, regulatory groups, professional societies, and visible vaccination champions, influenza vaccination rates among HCP remain unacceptably low."

The discouragingly low influenza vaccination rates among healthcare workers have prompted some healthcare facilities to consider mandatory influenza immunization for all staff.

INDIVIDUAL RIGHTS AND PROFESSIONALISM

Mandatory influenza immunization has met resistance from some healthcare workers. Resistance arises primarily from three concerns. First, some healthcare workers worry influenza vaccination could be harmful to their health (e.g., in the case of allergy to immunization). Second, some healthcare workers belong to faith groups that oppose medical interventions such as immunization. The third and perhaps most forceful argument for resistance centers on self-determination or autonomy—healthcare workers may resent being compelled to undergo immunization.

Each of these arguments prioritizes the single healthcare worker's individual rights. However, they do not take into consideration other key priorities such as the prevention of influenza epidemics or the principles of beneficence and nonmaleficence. Both of these cardinal bioethical principles suggest healthcare workers have a duty to act in the patient's interest and to avoid undue harm to patients.

While commonly applied to decision making around the provision of standard-of-care medical treatments, these principles can be interpreted to imply that healthcare workers have a moral duty to not place patients or colleagues at risk of preventable influenza infection. As noted in a September 2010 article by Andrew Miller, MD, and David Ross, MD, JD, in *Virtual Mentor,* the American Medical Association's ethics journal: "Applied to influenza vaccinations, this principle suggests that patients have the right to expect that their hospital will take every reasonable precaution to protect them from developing nosocomial illness."

How should healthcare executives balance these concerns? Are healthcare workers expected to undertake special risks to protect their patients from influenza? Is healthcare worker autonomy abbreviated by the desire to protect patients?

We believe the risks of influenza immunization are so small and manageable that mandatory influenza immunization cannot be faulted on patient safety grounds. An October 2010 Society for Healthcare Epidemiology of America position paper on this topic argues: "Because the likelihood of a serious adverse reaction to influenza vaccine is extremely low, the duty to protect vulnerable patients and to put their interest above the personal interest of the healthcare worker does not demand undue sacrifice." Furthermore, the very small risks flu shots present can be ameliorated by allowing healthcare workers with bona fide medical contraindications to immunization to opt out given adequate documentation of a valid risk.

There is a clear historical precedent for balancing the rights of healthcare workers (including the right to refuse immunization) with the interests of patients: Healthcare workers are routinely expected to provide standard-of-care treatments for contagious diseases and dangerous, unpleasant or indigent patients despite the potential for personal injury or the potential lack of monetary gain. For healthcare workers the primary duty is to patient care and safety.

This line of reasoning accords with the professional tenets of both clinicians and executives. Healthcare worker professionalism focuses on a commitment to their patients as the first priority. Patients expect this as a condition of public trust in the healthcare system and its providers.

DEVELOPING AND IMPLEMENTING A MANDATORY VACCINATION POLICY

Mandatory influenza immunization is controversial. As a result, many institutions attempted to prevent nosocomial influenza transmission via voluntary programs, which unfortunately resulted in a limited immunization uptick similar to the one seen in society in general. Given the greater vulnerability of hospitalized patients—and the ethical obligations of healthcare workers to those patients—we believe an ethically grounded policy of mandatory influenza vaccination is morally justified as long as implementation of the policy allows healthcare workers with medical or religious grounds to opt out.

Healthcare workers with medical or religious grounds for opting out should be made aware of a clearly delineated process that is easily available to stipulate and review their objection to influenza immunization and render a fair decision. The process should protect the confidentiality of the person seeking to opt out. The stated policy can stipulate a reasonable requirement that the healthcare worker document the justification for his or her objection, such as by providing a doctor's note to Human Resources specifying his or her medical contraindications to immunization or a letter stating a religious conviction and membership in a faith group that does not recognize vaccinations.

To ensure the opting-out process protects the rights of at-risk healthcare workers, and that it does not result in undermining of the purpose of mandatory influenza immunization through widespread, unsubstantiated opting out, there should be an objective review process. For instance, opt-out decisions should be made on the basis of standardized criteria that are applied systematically and not on a case-by-case basis. Furthermore, appeals to opt out should be reviewed by individuals who do not serve in a supervisory capacity for the healthcare worker in question.

Lastly, there should be a defined appeals process for the rare cases in which the healthcare worker does not accept the decision rendered by the institutional system. To ensure this system achieves the desired result of widespread healthcare worker immunization, we believe unfounded refusal of mandatory influenza immunization should be grounds for dismissal.

After the policy is drafted, reviewed and approved by the appropriate institutional clinical and administrative leaders and legal counsel, there needs to be a facilitywide effort to openly share the policy. Public conversation about the policy, if handled correctly, should help explain its rationale and identify routes of appeal for employees with a justified need to opt out.

In their February 15, 2010, article in the journal *Clinical Infectious Diseases*, Hilary Babcock and colleagues describe how their organization, BJC HealthCare, St. Louis, effectively communicated its immunization policy to employees as part of a broader patient safety initiative. This included disseminating the information through the organization's managers, educational materials, an in-house newsletter and town hall meetings. The key to their institution's success was strong leadership, a well-constructed policy and transparency regarding the ethical reasoning driving the policy, including the opting out mechanism. Following the implementation of any vaccination policy there should be regular and systematic assessment of the policy to determine if revisions are needed.

Despite being designed to protect vulnerable patients from preventable morbidity and mortality, mandatory influenza immunization is controversial. Opponents argue it subjects healthcare workers to unnecessary risks at the same time it infringes on their personal rights. We disagree.

The ethical principles of beneficence and nonmaleficence and the application of professionalism dictate that healthcare workers should take reasonable steps to prevent influenza in vulnerable patients. Given the proven efficacy of and low risks associated with influenza immunization, a mandatory influenza immunization system with a fair and objective opt-out process is the ethical approach to the prevention of influenza-related mortality and morbidity in healthcare facilities.

Originally published in the November/December 2013 issue of *Healthcare Executive* magazine.

Discussion Questions

The proposal to mandate flu vaccination for healthcare professionals is controversial due to the moral consideration of depriving people of their right of choice. What justification can a leader apply to make such a requirement? If you believe there are valid reasons to allow exemptions, what are they?

Opponents of mandating flu or COVID-19 vaccination for healthcare staff argue that such a requirement infringes on their personal rights. What reasons would justify the dismissal of a staff member who continued to refuse vaccination?

Proposed Ethics Guidelines for Quality Improvement

William A. Nelson, PhD, HFACHE

DURING THE LAST FEW decades there has been growing recognition of the importance of quality improvement interventions to ensure healthcare is effectively and efficiently delivered. Many healthcare organizations have created improvement offices and identified improvement leaders to foster these efforts. The result has led to the implementation of countless improvement initiatives to enhance the quality of patient care. For example, a hospital implemented and assessed an approach to obtain advance directives. Another hospital implemented and assessed the use of a checklist to reduce central line infections in its intensive care unit.

Similar to ethical issues arising in human subject research, ethical issues can arise in QI activities. However, unlike with research, there has been limited focus on creating ethical guidelines for QI activities.

The development of ethical requirements for human subject research grew out of scandals surrounding human experimentation. Morally repugnant research was not only carried out during World War II—there also have been hundreds of unethical research studies conducted in the United States. The public and scientific community's recognition of unethical research was a driver for the development of formal ethical standards and codes of ethics to guide human subject research.

Even though there have been no scandals involving quality improvement activities, there certainly are situations when QI activities create ethical concerns. For example, because QI activities are data-guided interventions designed to bring improvement to specific settings, using an inappropriate methodology to achieve the stated goals will render the resulting findings meaningless. Such a situation is an ethical concern because of the wasted resources resulting from use of an inappropriate methodology.

QI activities can create harm when privacy and confidentiality are breached or have unfairly affected patients. Furthermore, the lack of a clearly applied distinction between QI and research along with the lack of QI ethical standards serves as an incentive for some to designate a research study as a QI activity, thus circumventing the more rigorous research review process. The extent of this problem is not known, yet it does present another ethical concern.

As a result of both the sheer growth of QI activities and the potential for patient privacy breaches, wasted resources and violations in professional integrity, there is support for the need to ensure QI activities be conducted within the context of ethical behavior. These activities ought to be facilitated and monitored within the context of an ethical framework to protect participants and the validity of the activity.

CREATING AN ETHICAL FRAMEWORK FOR QI ACTIVITIES

For quite some time there was no comprehensive description of an ethical framework for QI activities. However, that has changed. A group of clinicians, improvement leaders, ethicists and other healthcare professionals authored an important manuscript proposing requirements for the ethical conduct of quality improvement. The suggested ethical requirements were offered in an article in the May 1, 2007, issue of *Annals of Internal Medicine* by Joanne Lynn,

MD, and colleagues. The authors' suggested requirements include that a QI activity have:

- Social or scientific value—The anticipated improvement from the QI activity should justify the effort in the use of time and resources.
- Scientific validity—The QI activity must be methodologically sound.
- Fair patient selection—The participants in the QI activity should be selected to achieve fairness in the benefits and burdens of the intervention.
- Favorable benefit/risk ratio—The QI activity should limit risks, such as privacy and confidentiality, and maximize benefits to participants.
- Respect for participants—The QI activity is designed to protect patients' confidentiality and make them aware of findings relevant to their care. Also, participants should receive basic information regarding the activity.
- Informed consent—When the activity is more than minimum risk, informed consent should be sought.
- Independent review—The proposed activity should be reviewed to ensure it meets the ethical standards in place.

STRATEGIES FOR REVIEWING QI ACTIVITIES

As described in the suggested ethical framework, there is a need to thoughtfully and systematically review quality improvement activities to ensure they meet the ethical framework for QI. Unlike the federally required institutional review boards (IRBs) that assess and monitor research protocols, there currently is no required mechanism for providing review and oversight of QI activities.

Despite the lack of a federal requirement, healthcare leaders should ensure QI interventions conform to an ethical framework to protect patients and foster the integrity of the organization. To achieve independent review of QI activities, several issues need to be addressed.

First, what is the appropriate mechanism by which to conduct the review for your organization? To date there is no uniformly applied mechanism or procedure for reviewing QI activities. For some institutions the review is facilitated within the clinical department or section. In other settings the ethical review might be facilitated by the QI office or an independent advisory board. Unfortunately, in many organizations there is no review.

The lack of an established review structure and process can create problems for both quality improvement professionals and the organization. For example, requiring a QI activity to be reviewed forces a healthcare professional to draft a protocol for the proposed improvement activity. The sheer process of thinking through the activity in terms of its goal, design method, intended benefit, potential risk, assessment of findings and dissemination of findings enhances the credibility of the QI activity and prevents poorly developed interventions from being implemented. The level of review, similar to the review of research protocols, will relate to potential risks or burdens of the QI activity. Despite the lack of a uniform QI ethical review model, it needs to be conducted in every facility by professionals who are knowledgeable in both quality improvement and ethics.

Related to this structural issue is the frequently encountered problem related to the difference between QI and human subject research. Because IRB members do not have the time, the interest nor the QI expertise to review QI activities, there needs to be a consistently applied approach to differentiating between a human subject research initiative and a QI one. Unfortunately, healthcare professionals, QI professionals, researchers and IRB members do not agree on the distinction.

For years the distinction focused on whether the findings would be published; if an activity was going to be published, it was research. Appropriately, that criterion for making the distinction has been fading. For example, *VHA Handbook 1058.05,* October 2011, notes, "Publication or presentation outside VA of findings from non-research operations activities . . . does not, in and of itself, constitute research." However, inconsistency remains prevalent in making the distinction between research and QI activities. I suspect that if a healthcare system has various facilities, variation exists among the various facilities in their approach to distinguishing QI initiatives from research.

Even if a QI review mechanism does exist, the likelihood of organization-wide consistency in differentiating between research and QI is small. This is particularly challenging because there are activities that are pure research—such as randomized clinical trials to assess a new medication—just as there are pure QI activities, such as an intervention to decrease patient wait time in a specific outpatient clinic.

However, there are activities that fall in the middle territory, such as a multi-institutional study of a checklist to improve the efficiency and safety of colonoscopy procedures.

To assist in distinguishing between QI and clinical research, Greg Ogrinc, myself and colleagues published "An Instrument to Differentiate Between Clinical Research and Quality Improvement" in the September/October 2013 issue of *IRB: Ethics & Human Research.* In the article we offer a checklist that can be used by IRB members, QI review staff, researchers and quality improvement professionals to increase consistency in determining whether a particular protocol is to be reviewed by the IRB or through the organization's QI review mechanism.

The screening instrument starts with four basic questions addressing important considerations in making the assessment, including considering if the activity is within the standard of care. A "no" response to that question would be a strong indicator that the activity should be IRB reviewed. Following these basic questions, the instrument lists six attributes that further distinguish research from QI. Next to each of the six attributes are two columns: one for QI and the other for research. Each column lists characteristics that are consistent with research ethics regulations and the proposed QI ethics framework for the attribute. If any item is checked in the clinical research column, then the proposal is likely research and ought to be reviewed by the IRB. If any of the items are checked in the QI column, then the proposal should be reviewed according to the organization's QI review mechanism.

The tool is not an absolute adjudicator, but it is helpful in framing a discussion and confidence regarding these decisions. Early pilot findings have verified the value of the research-QI checklist instrument. Such a checklist could benefit healthcare organizations' need for a consistently applied understanding of what is research and what is QI, leading to the appropriate review mechanism.

RECOMMENDATIONS FOR ACTION

Healthcare executives need to recognize not only the importance of quality improvement activities but the need to foster such activities within the context of an ethical framework. Fundamental to the ethical framework is the requirement to systematically review and monitor QI interventions.

Because there is no one best model for ensuring the QI activity is conducted in an ethical manner, healthcare executives should determine in consultation with quality improvement professionals and research professionals what is the most appropriate internal management mechanism and process for their organization. The creation of a process for QI ethics review could contribute to the quality of QI intervention and prevention of unethical activities.

Originally published in the March/April 2014 issue of *Healthcare Executive* magazine.

Discussion Questions

Describe the potential risks or harms in conducting quality improvement interventions that may create ethical concerns.

The author proposed the creation of a QI review mechanism applying an ethical framework. How might a quality improvement intervention for human subjects' research require a different review process?

Rethinking the Traditional Ethics Committee

William A. Nelson, PhD, HFACHE

ETHICS COMMITTEES ARE A well-recognized resource in health-care institutions. In an acknowledgment of their importance, The Joint Commission established standards requiring an "ethics mechanism" to address ethical conflicts. As a result, the vast majority of hospitals in the United States have ethics committees that focus primarily on clinical ethics challenges, namely those issues and conflicts that relate specifically to patient care.

Important to note is that issues will arise that are primarily organizational but also have clinical ramifications. Some examples include organizational actions regarding downsizing and mergers. Each activity raises a multitude of ethics issues that require thoughtful ethical reflection.

Another organizational issue that calls for ethics reflection on both the clinical and organizational sides is the development of accountable care organizations. The ACO model aims to reduce healthcare costs and improve quality and patient satisfaction by offering financial incentives to providers for integrating a range of health services systems. The goal of this coordinated care is to ensure patients receive the right care at the right time while avoiding unnecessary duplication of services and unnecessary interventions.

The implementation of ACOs, however, raises ethical challenges for healthcare executives and clinicians. Federal ACO guidelines include the Medicare Shared Savings Program, in which providers and organizations will be paid more by keeping their patients healthy and out of the hospital. How will ACOs address the potential conflicts of interest for clinicians and organizational leaders created by the incentives for shared savings? Could a perception of conflict of interest undermine the clinician–patient relationship? Again, healthcare executives need to acknowledge the presence of not only clinical but also organizational ethics issues.

Executives, like physicians, also need to see ethics programs as useful resources for fulfilling their tasks of leading mission- and value-based organizations. As Jim Sabin, MD, director of the Harvard Pilgrim Health Care Ethics Program, has stated, when the CEO does not see himself as the chief ethics officer, there is little hope that organizational ethics will be addressed, regardless of whether the CEO is a member of the expanded ethics committee.

No universal model exists for expanding ethics committees to include organizational ethics, as noted in a previous *Healthcare Executive* column (March/April 2008). Some organizations that have tested the water in terms of addressing organizational ethics issues have done so by creating a separate committee; others have addressed clinical and organizational ethics issues as part of the operations of a single committee. Each organization must assess which approach best meets its unique needs; I most often see greater advantage gained by one committee capable of addressing both.

GUIDELINES FOR INCLUDING ORGANIZATIONAL ETHICS ISSUES

In the summer 2016 issue of the *Journal of Clinical Ethics,* Sabin offers practical guidelines for clinical ethics committees moving to include organizational ethics. First, educate committee members about various administrative functions, such as payment models, financial management, human resources, compliance regulations and laws.

Second, build clear relationships with administrative leaders, for example, by exploring which administrative issues might benefit from an ethics review process. Relationship building is a matter of committee members developing a linkage with executives through face-to-face dialogue, allowing executives to see the ethics committee as an ally and a competent resource available to assist leadership in addressing the complex challenges they face.

Third, the committee should broaden its membership to include staff from administration. Not only can these staff members bring their unique insights when the committee is reflecting on organizational issues, but their participation also is a way to build trust and respect between the committee and the C-suite.

And fourth, Sabin suggests committees move slowly and avoid a "fix-it" approach. As Sabin notes, with "organizational ethics, which is much less understood and established than clinical ethics, having the committee spend time educating itself, developing relationships, and piloting the consultation process before it launches 'for real' will be time well spent."

The presence of ethical challenges related to organizational decisions and actions emphasizes the need for a comprehensive and capable ethics committee similar to that used to address clinical issues. Just as healthcare delivery is changing, the traditional model of a hospital-based clinical ethics committee must evolve.

For ethics committees and programs to effectively serve an important role for healthcare organizations and leaders, policy-makers and others, they will need to review and likely revise their traditional role in today's healthcare environment. An expanded role, focusing on the overlap of clinical and organizational issues, is essential to ensure changes in healthcare delivery reflect our common ethical concepts for health and healthcare.

Originally published in the January/February 2017 issue of *Healthcare Executive* magazine.

Discussion Questions

Traditional ethics committees have focused on clinical ethics challenges, that is, conflicts occurring within the context of specific patient care situations. How are organizational ethics challenges different?

What additional areas of knowledge and skills do members of traditional clinical ethics committees need to possess to address organizational ethics conflicts?

Discrimination and Patient-Centered Care

William A. Nelson, PhD, HFACHE,
and Andrew Huang, MD

TODAY'S HEALTHCARE ORGANIZATIONS HAVE embraced the concept of patient-centered care, ensuring that clinical care is respectful and responsive to individual patient preferences, needs and values. Patient-centered care is epitomized by shared decision making between patients and clinical care teams. Adding further weight to the patient-centered care aim is its linkage to a basic ethical concept underpinning the delivery of healthcare: respect for patients' autonomy. Achieving patient-centered care and adhering to the principle of autonomy are foundational to the success of any clinician–patient encounter.

ACHE's *Code of Ethics*

The ACHE *Code of Ethics* is clear in its expectations for healthcare executives in terms of discrimination. In relationship to the executives' responsibility to employees, "There is zero tolerance for bigotry." Healthcare leaders are called to promote "a culture of inclusivity that seeks to prevent discrimination on the basis of race, ethnicity, religion, gender, sexual orientation, age or disability." In relationship to executives' responsibilities to the clinical setting, they are to "avoid practicing or facilitating discrimination and institute safeguards to prevent discriminatory organizational practices."

With the emphasis on patient-centered care has come related ethical concerns that ask the question, are there limits to a patient's autonomy? Many of those concerns have focused on problems related to end-of-life decision making, such as medical futility, when patients or family members demand interventions that are contrary to the standard of care or to the patient's advance directive. However, other situations center on whether limiting patient autonomy is justifiable.

The same basic dilemma regarding the scope of patient autonomy relates to patients who demand that their healthcare provider be of a certain race or ethnic group. The issue can manifest itself in a variety of clinical scenarios, ranging from requests that seem quite reasonable to those that are questionable or flagrantly racist. The American College of Physicians' Ethics Manual affirms that "a patient is free to change physicians at any time." The American Medical Association's *Code of Medical Ethics* similarly affirms a patient's right "to a second opinion" and "reasonable assistance in making alternative arrangements for care," if changing care. It is understandable, for example, for a woman to request a female gynecologist or a male to request a male physician for his colonoscopy. To the extent possible, hospitals should try to accommodate such reasonable requests, whether they are based on religious beliefs, cultural norms or personal values.

DISCRIMINATION'S EFFECT ON STAFF

However, other types of patient requests or demands regarding their choice of caregiver seem less ethically clear. One example is when a patient demands that his or her caregiver be of a specific race due to racist beliefs. Consider a white male patient who demands that his ED physician not be African-American or a Christian female who requests that no caregivers of Muslim faith be involved in her care while in the hospital. Once, in a rural outpatient clinic, a white, bipolar patient dismissed Andrew Huang and, in her growing impatience and anxiety, yelled "I don't want to see some stupid Chinese student!" She then demanded to be seen by a specific doctor. Discrimination in healthcare is an unpleasant topic. Yet, like other disturbing issues that resonate in our society, we need to address discrimination's impact on clinical care and the delivery of healthcare. When a patient requests a different provider out of bigotry, how far must clinicians and healthcare organizations go to fulfill that request?

A 2014 *JAMA* article by Meghan Lane-Fall, MD, a female African-American critical care doctor, poignantly describes a physician's experience with a bigoted patient's demands, as well as the "befuddled" looks from her patients that she was a physician. However, as Lane-Fall notes, "my discomfort with the patient's beliefs does not trump their right to specify the conditions of their care."

Such situations raise challenging ethical and legal issues and affect the caregiver–patient relationship. Hospitals that stipulate policy that requires clinicians to fulfill such patient requests pose a dilemma, as a hospital leader would neither want to condone discrimination nor allow doctors to fail to provide appropriate care.

In addition, hospital caregivers may experience moral distress when a patient expresses preferences based on discriminatory thinking. The presence of moral distress can have a major impact on morale and staff burnout. For example, how do hospitals support a gay nurse who is facing burnout as a result of continued moral distress over repetitive verbal abuse received from homophobic patients?

ORGANIZATIONAL RESPONSE TO DISCRIMINATION

Because these sorts of encounters occur in the context of a healthcare organization, administrative and clinical leaders have an important role to play in addressing this concern. Specifically, organizational leaders need to learn and recognize the many ethical and legal issues surrounding race-based patient demands, develop thoughtful practice guidelines for responding to such requests and assess the impact of those guidelines. The creation of guidelines should take place within a thoughtful process involving many professionals from a variety of disciplines. Practice guidelines can unify responses in patient-care decisions and contribute to staff morale by offering a comprehensive approach for responding to these situations.

Kiimani Paul-Emile, JD, PhD, and colleagues, in a February 25, 2016, article in the *New England Journal of Medicine*, describe a useful starting framework for developing organizational practice guidelines regarding the management of a situation involving a racist patient. They focus on five elements to help direct whether to accommodate a bigoted request: the patient's medical stability, decision-making capacity and reasons for the request; the organization's ability to accommodate; and the impact of the request on the medical team.

Their guidelines describe clear cases involving either patients who are medically stable or those who lack decision-making capacity. For example, if a bigoted patient with decision-making capacity is medically unstable and in need of immediate care, timely treatment takes priority. However, Paul-Emile and colleagues note, if a stable but racist patient lacks decision-making capacity, clinicians should attempt to persuade and negotiate care approaches to treat the patient.

Guidelines for Addressing Discrimination Among Patients

- Recognize that discrimination exists in the delivery of healthcare and that it creates moral stress and uncertainty for staff.
- Develop practice guidelines to assist clinicians. The guidelines should be carefully written based on the thoughtful advice of legal counsel, an ethics committee, human resources, administration and clinician services representatives. Practice guidelines can promote a consistent response to discriminatory demands.
- Develop an education program to familiarize staff with the ethical and legal underpinning of the practice guidelines. Training should cover how to effectively communicate

and negotiate with patients who express discriminatory demands.

- Ensure that helpful resources, such as an ethics committee or risk-management staff, are readily available when clinicians face challenging situations.
- Assess the practice guidelines and any related programs to determine if they foster a consistent ethically and legally grounded approach to patient-entered care and address staff's uncertainty and stress. Whenever such a patient encounter occurs, a retrospective review should be undertaken to evaluate what was done well and what could have been better. This evaluation process can improve future patient–staff encounters when the issue recurs. It also benefits the involved parties and creates a culture of open reflection.

A medically stable patient with decision-making capacity who makes a racist request presents a more difficult set of concerns. A key factor in determining whether to accommodate is the availability of resources. Some healthcare settings, such as small, rural or critical access hospitals, have limited medical personnel and resources to meet this demand. A medically stable patient can accept the available resources or agree to be transferred to another facility that can accommodate the demand.

Another potential disqualifier for accommodation is when a stable patient absolutely refuses to negotiate or compromise his or her discriminatory position and is verbally abusive in the exchange. If all staff approaches for accommodation have been exhausted, the patient has been warned not to abuse staff and he or she continues to be uncooperative, then the patient may be deemed as undeserving of a replacement caregiver.

Despite the useful strategy expressed by Paul-Emile and colleagues, they indicate, "No ethical duty is absolute, and reasonable limits may be placed on unacceptable patient conduct."

Unfortunately, no algorithm can provide easy answers to these complex clinician scenarios.

The concept of patient-centered healthcare is challenged by discriminatory patient demands. Healthcare professionals have an ethical responsibility to ensure that patients receive needed care. As frustrating as it may be for clinical staff, meeting the patient's healthcare need may include attempting to accommodate the patient's discriminatory demand by transferring the patient to another provider. Organizational practice guidelines can provide ethical and legal guidance to caregivers for identifying and resolving those rare situations in which refusing discriminatory requests is justified.

Originally published in the March/April 2017 issue of *Healthcare Executive* magazine.

Discussion Questions

Patient autonomy suggests that patients can choose their healthcare provider, even if the choice is based on the provider's race. Describe situations where there may be a moral justification for not accepting a patient's choice.

The authors suggest that healthcare institutions should have formal policies related to patients' discriminatory demands. Why is there a need for such policies?

The Debate Over Aid-in-Dying Laws

Paul B. Hofmann, DrPH, LFACHE

AFTER YEARS OF DEBATE on this difficult and complex moral issue, on June 9, 2016, California became the sixth state in the nation to allow physicians to prescribe terminally ill patients medication to end their lives. The End of Life Option Act permits terminally ill adult patients with decision-making capacity to make medical decisions to be prescribed an aid-in-dying medication if certain conditions are met. Patients can qualify when they:

- Are over the age of 18
- Have a prognosis of six months or less to live as confirmed by two physicians
- Have made two oral requests to their attending physician, separated by at least 15 days
- Provide the physician with a written request, including signatures from witnesses
- Have the physician assess their mental capacity to assure that they are choosing freely and intentionally and are informed of alternative options
- Speak to the physician alone on at least one occasion to confirm there is no possibility of coercion by others
- Can self-administer the prescribed drug

Oregon (1997), Washington (2008), Montana (2009 via a State Supreme Court decision), Vermont (2013), Colorado (2016), Washington, D.C. (2017) and, most recently, Hawaii (2018) are the other jurisdictions that allow physicians to prescribe medication to the terminally ill to end their lives.

Given that at least 30 additional states have introduced similar legislation, hospital executives should be prepared to facilitate an informed discussion about an institution's position if a comparable law is approved.

CONTENTIOUS MORAL DEBATE CONTINUES

As with most controversial issues, even the basic terminology used in discussing the topic is value-laden. Opponents invariably refer to assisted suicide, and proponents usually talk about death with dignity, assisted dying or assisted death and note the act taken by a patient is not legally classified as a suicide. The patient's terminal disease is listed as the cause of death.

Opponents base their objections upon deeply held moral convictions. Physicians and others opposing the concept argue vigorously that it is inherently antithetical to the Hippocratic Oath, the admonition to do no harm and the healthcare professional's obligation to preserve, extend and protect the sanctity of life. Supporters emphasize that death is not the enemy; needless suffering is.

During Oregon's legislative debate of its Death with Dignity Act, despite ultimately successful efforts to significantly limit the number of terminally ill patients eligible to request medication to end their lives, serious concerns were raised suggesting that the proposed law represented the first step along a "slippery slope" leading to mercy killing and the death of vulnerable members of society with physical and/or mental disabilities.

Critics express concern that at least three countries, the Netherlands, Belgium and Switzerland, allow assisted deaths for people who have severe psychiatric problems. Those who endorse assisted death legislation in the U.S. unequivocally insist that they are extremely sensitive to the slippery slope suggestion, saying it is simply unwarranted to even imply that comparable proposals would be acceptable here. According to an article in the August 3, 2017, issue of *The New England Journal of Medicine* titled, "End-of-Life Decisions in the Netherlands over 25 Years," aid-in-dying has represented 0.1 percent of end-of-life practices from 1990 to 2015, and the figure has remained consistent during this period.

Canada, Luxembourg and the Australian state of Victoria also have passed physician aid-in-dying legislation, which other countries are considering as well.

In September 2017, the American College of Physicians issued a position paper stating it does not support legalization of physician-assisted suicide because, in part, "It is problematic given the nature of the patient–physician relationship, affects trust in the relationship and in the profession, and fundamentally alters the medical profession's role in society."

Writing in the October 17, 2017, issue of the *Annals of Internal Medicine*, two members of the Oregon Health Authority stated the questions around the debate fell into two broad categories. "First, do statutory safeguards protect vulnerable patients? Are participating patients disproportionately poor or uneducated, or do they have financial concerns? Do patients participate because they lack access to health insurance or palliative care? Are they depressed?" Second, the authors asked if such laws are ethical, do they interfere with the patient–physician relationship and do they devalue human life?

Regarding Oregon's experience, innumerable studies have been conducted to evaluate not only how many patients made requests and met the eligibility prerequisites but also the number and characteristics of patients who actually took the medication. In the *Annals of Internal Medicine* report, the latter figures have been lower than anticipated. From 1998 through June 2017, 1,857 Oregonians received aid-in-dying prescriptions, and 64 percent died from taking the medication. In 2016, physician-assisted deaths accounted for 37 per 10,000 deaths in Oregon, according to the "California End of

Life Option Act 2016 Data Report," published by the California Department of Public Health.

They represented six out of every 10,000 deaths in California between June and December 2016, a figure certainly likely to rise because the law was still relatively new.

In addition to other information, Oregon and California collect data on the patient's diagnosis, age, ethnicity and education. The majority in both states had cancer, were over 60, white and college-educated.

Understandably, Oregon has the largest database, including information on the most common reasons for choosing aid-in-dying: fear of loss of autonomy (91 percent), being less able to engage in activities that made life enjoyable (89 percent), burdening family or caregivers (41 percent), and worries about pain control (25 percent). Particularly noteworthy is that 88 percent of all patients were already receiving hospice services.

Advocates have highlighted the ethical principle of patient autonomy, emphasizing the right of self-determination should include the ability to maintain control over a key decision.

Although there is an apparent trend toward physician aid-in-dying, it is quite evident that many people legitimately question whether it is ethical and necessary. As mentioned previously, some have said it simply demonstrates the U.S. healthcare system's failure to provide proper access to effective palliative care.

However, as mentioned in a review in *The New England Journal of Medicine,* March 16, 2017, issue, "The legalization of assisted death has been associated with substantial improvements in palliative care in Oregon, in areas including the appropriate training of physicians, the communication of a patient's wishes regarding life-sustaining treatment, pain management, rates of referral to hospice programs and the percentage of deaths occurring at home."

Hospital executives may be concerned that a significant number of patients may choose to self-administer the medication in the hospital. In fact, such occurrences are extremely rare. Over 99 percent of patients in Oregon who took the lethal medication did so in their homes or non-hospital settings.

DEVELOPING AN OBJECTIVE APPROACH

Because a number of states may adopt legislation comparable to California and other parts of the country, hospital executives should monitor developments and, if a similar law is passed, design a process that seeks participation by a variety of key stakeholders in determining the organization's role. Executives also should be mindful that Catholic and faith-based institutions represent the clear majority of health systems and hospitals that have chosen to opt out of participation.

Among the major steps for consideration are the following:

1. Educate board members, physicians and employees about the law.

2. Identify how the diverse perspectives of physicians, board members, management and the community will be accommodated.

3. Emphasize the hospital's strong commitment to supporting patient-centered decision making and a process that gives highest priority to each patient's preferences and values.

4. Leverage the cumulative experience of hospitals that have opted in and out of participation in jurisdictions with aid-in-dying legislation.

5. Assure physicians and employees that conscientious objection to participation with aid-in-dying will be honored if the hospital opts into the program.

6. Initiate programs to inform the public of the law and the hospital's position.

7. Encourage the hospital to neither promote nor discourage patients' involvement in assisted dying.

8. Designate the ethics committee as a central resource for reviewing best practices and developing appropriate policies and procedures, subject to approval by senior management, the medical staff and board if the hospital opts in.

Regardless of the institution's ultimate decision, the executive's responsibility is to ensure it will be consistent with the hospital's vision, mission and values. We can expect competent and compassionate people to express disparate views about such an important topic. The ultimate goal is to achieve consensus based on conversations characterized by mutual trust and confidence that the debate was inclusive and respectful.

Originally published in the July/August 2018 issue of *Healthcare Executive* magazine.

Discussion Questions

Comment on the provocative and important questions raised in the two broad categories described in the October 17, 2017, issue of the *Annals of Internal Medicine* referenced on page 95.

Considering that every executive will have a personal view on this ethically complex issue, how should they participate in discussions without compromising their beliefs and values?

The Ethical Foundation for Environmental Responsibility

John J. Donnellan Jr., FACHE,
and Cassandra Thiel, PhD

HEALTHCARE PROVIDERS KNOW THAT the global environment affects health, but few realize the sizable negative effect healthcare services have on the environment. Providing medical care requires massive amounts of resources, particularly for hospitalizations and surgical procedures. Hospitals are the second most energy-intensive buildings in the U.S. and consumed more than 450 trillion British thermal units of energy in 2007, according to the U.S. Energy Information Administration 2012 report, *Commercial Buildings Energy Consumption Survey*, the most recent data available.

Medical procedures in the U.S. and in other developed countries use a large number of devices and materials that in turn generate large quantities of waste. The medical supply chain accounts for 30–40 percent of a hospital's expenses. Considering the cost of procurement, storage and other factors, activities in the supply chain can account for 50 percent of an organization's budget, according to the 2009 *Healthcare Financial Management* article "Needed: A strategic approach to supply chain management: hospital senior financial executives need to recalculate the strategic significance of the supply chain—and plan accordingly."

Because most medical supplies are single-use and disposable, they ultimately end up in our medical waste streams. In its *2016 Sustainability Benchmark Report*, environmental organization Practice Greenhealth states that by conservative estimates, U.S. hospitals generate more than 4.7 million tons of waste annually, or 27 pounds-per-staffed hospital bed per day.

Resource use generates emissions as well, as energy sources are extracted and burned and products are manufactured and shipped all around the world. Within the last two years, articles in both the *American Journal of Public Health* and the *Journal of Hospital Medicine* have reported estimates that the U.S. healthcare system generates approximately 10 percent of U.S. greenhouse gases. If the U.S. healthcare system were a country, it would be the 13th largest emitter of greenhouse gases in the world.

Striving for resource efficiency, however, and the reduction of waste in medicine has not been a priority.

DO WE HAVE AN ETHICAL OBLIGATION TO ACT?

Considering the volume and kinds of waste produced by healthcare organizations, what should be the expectation of healthcare organization leaders? Is being a responsible steward of our environment an obligation of healthcare organizational leaders? Is it an ethical obligation? To what extent must we understand the volume of waste we produce and take steps to reduce or eliminate the environmental harm that's caused?

The ACHE *Code of Ethics* states that healthcare executives provide patients and staff alike a safe and healthy work environment and assess how strategic choices affect both the community served and society as a whole. The ethical principle of nonmaleficence demands that providers do no harm. Most often, the principle of nonmaleficence is applied to avoiding unnecessary harm to individuals, but some argue that it applies equally to avoiding harm to society; to not depriving others of the goods of life, according to *Principles of Biomedical Ethics* (Oxford University Press, 2013).

The principle of social and distributive justice requires a utilitarian approach—a need to strike a balance between benefit to an individual or a group (beneficence) and potential harm to others.

We argue that this also extends to harming the community and the global environment. Perhaps a 2012 issue of *The New England Journal of Medicine* best captures the point: We have an ethical obligation to avoid unnecessary waste.

WHO IS DOING IT WELL?

In two separate journal articles, the authors reported on the implementation of very efficient ophthalmologic surgical processes at Aravind Eye Care System in India. By adopting a "McDonalds" approach to eye care, Aravind created a safe and high-quality system for cataract and other eye surgeries that resulted in better access, lower carbon emissions and lower costs. Some of Aravind's processes do not comply with U.S. regulations and would need modification, but some practices merit examination.

Kaiser Permanente, Oakland, California, was an early adopter of comprehensive sustainability and environmental stewardship. Kaiser has set ambitious sustainability targets for 2025 that include becoming carbon-net positive, reducing water usage by 25 percent, practicing local food sourcing, and recycling, and reusing or composting 100 percent of its nonhazardous wastes. In addition, Kaiser released a sustainability scorecard, requiring its suppliers to provide environmental data on the products Kaiser purchased.

Cleveland Clinic is a signatory of the United Nations Global Compact, supporting the 2030 Sustainable Development Goals. As such, it publicly reports its performance against goals, while also reporting to the Global Reporting Initiative. It has stated goals to reduce carbon emissions, save energy and work with suppliers in creating greener medical products and supplies.

Small healthcare systems also can get involved. Gundersen Health, La Crosse, Wisconsin, developed an energy program to reduce energy needs and to source all energy locally. It also is working on reducing food waste.

WHAT CAN YOU DO?

The first thing you can do is be aware of the problem and start monitoring your organization. Begin by simply understanding the resources your facility uses. How much garbage do you generate? How much do you spend on supply purchasing and waste disposal? How much electricity do you use? How does this compare to medical facilities of similar size? Do any particular services generate inordinate amounts of waste or use more resources than they should?

Second, take small steps to reduce waste. A survey of waste from 58 neurosurgical procedures performed at a large academic hospital found that, on average, 13 percent of surgical supplies went unused, at a total cost of $968 per case and an estimated annual cost of $2.9 million for the neurosurgical department, according to a 2016 article in the *Journal of Neurosurgery.* Variation in care delivery among physicians can result in a range of surgical supply costs and wasted, unused materials.

Third, take steps to engage your employees and find partners and motivators. Make waste reduction part of the organizational culture and statement of values. Encourage the establishment of waste-reduction strategies and performance targets at departmental levels, and create financial and nonfinancial incentives for achieving them. The implementation of sustainability initiatives can occur at virtually any level, from chefs in the kitchens to nurses in the OR; pharmacists preparing solutions or lab techs prepping samples; housekeeping turning over an inpatient bed; and your administrative assistant scheduling your next meeting. Find a balance between goals and resources (funding, labor), and ensure that all are data-driven. There are national and international groups that can provide ideas for sustainability strategies, management structures and specific interventions.

Lastly, your industry partners within the supply chain are a crucial resource in sustainability efforts.

Hospitals and healthcare organizations provide an enormous public good, but many tend to ignore the impact they have on the environment. Embracing our responsibility to be good stewards of the environment is the ethical responsibility of those who lead healthcare organizations. It also is good for business.

Originally published in the January/February 2019 issue of *Healthcare Executive* magazine.

Discussion Questions

Given the growing concern about the impact of climate change, suggest some reasons for the lack of more creative initiatives by healthcare organizations.

If healthcare organizations must be better stewards of our environment, which examples and recommendations cited in the article do you believe will be most effective and why?

Ethical Considerations When Treating VIPs

John J. Donnellan Jr., FACHE

I OFTEN FIND MYSELF in conversations with students who work in healthcare as clinicians, administrators or support personnel about the moral conflict they experience when attending to "special patients," often referred to as "VIPs" (very important or very influential patients). This occurs frequently in large urban areas that are home to internationally renowned academic medical centers (such as New York City, where I live and work), but it is by no means a situation occurring exclusively in those cities, and the moral distress staff experience is no less real.

The same conflict often arises in community hospitals, where staff members may be conflicted about perceived differences in care provided to elected officials, business leaders, hospital benefactors and other well-known individuals. Indeed, the distress is often mitigated in large urban medical centers, which are more likely to have hospital units specially designed to provide VIP care in highly private settings.

The moral distress and ethical conflict that staff members express is grounded in a deep appreciation of the ethical principle of justice as it applies to the delivery of healthcare. Justice demands that all individuals seeking care are treated as equals, regardless of fortune, fame, social position, occupation or influence. That some patients may wait far longer for appointments or be held on a gurney in an ED while the more famous and well-to-do are quickly whisked away to a luxurious setting is viewed by many as unfair and indefensible. That said, most appreciate how vital it is to assure all patients privacy, confidentiality and dignity, and understand how difficult doing so can be if the patient is a focus, for whatever reason, of intense media interest or simple curiosity by persons without the need or right to know.

WHO IS A VIP?

Although healthcare workers agree that every patient is a VIP, for this discussion we will focus on the care of individuals who by virtue of celebrity, wealth, social status or influence (perceived or actual) are attended to in a special way. They may be treated in very private and luxuriously appointed areas of the institution, provided with amenities more akin to a five-star hotel than a hospital, and scheduled for appointments, procedures and consultations much more discreetly and expeditiously, as highlighted in a January 2012 *New York Times* article, "Chefs, Butlers, Marble Baths: Hospitals Vie for the Affluent." The VIPs may not only be the rich and famous. Questions to consider include, are the organization's board members, influential donors, community leaders or senior leaders and their families given preferential treatment? If so, is the difference only in privacy and amenities, or does it extend to decisions about who provides care, how and where it is provided, and, ultimately, clinical judgment and care quality?

The Joint Commission standard LD.04.03.07 specifies that:

- Patients with comparable needs receive the same standard of care, treatment and services throughout the hospital.
- Variances in staff, setting or payment source do not affect outcomes of care, treatment and services in a negative way.

Some will argue that the setting and amenities that surround the provision of care absolutely affect outcome. Others point out that multiple factors beyond the hospital's control may influence care outcomes. These dynamics include the patient's personal wealth, the quality and stability of living situations to which patients are discharged, and access to a wide range of post-hospital care and rehabilitation. Many also point to the larger community benefit that may result from providing special care to a VIP, noting revenue sources for the institution that are far more substantial than typical negotiated insurance rates, and the ability to raise public awareness about medical conditions that are underfunded, underreported, undertreated and poorly understood.

IS VIP CARE BETTER CARE?

VIP care may involve risks that outweigh advantages. As noted by the authors in the article "Ethical considerations in clinical care of the 'VIP'" in the spring 2007 issue of the *Journal of Clinical Ethics*—which remains relevant today—routine examinations, such as complete history and physical exam, may be less than thorough, and informed consent may be compromised or incomplete. The VIP may be at risk for overtreatment or undertreatment, and accommodating a VIP's unrealistic demands for procedures, treatments or medications may prove harmful to the individual's health. The desire to ensure that a VIP is seen by the highest-ranking clinician can result in delayed care and, in the end, not being cared for by the most qualified clinician.

Preferential care can result in negative consequences to other patients, too. VIPs granted special scheduling may result in delays in the diagnosis of other patients. Failing to recognize the moral distress staff members experience when caring for VIPs may result in decreased staff morale and a sense that the organization's stated mission, vision and values do not matter.

ETHICAL CONSIDERATIONS IN THE MANAGEMENT AND DELIVERY OF VIP CARE

The *Journal of Clinical Ethics* article recommends the following be acknowledged and considered when providing VIP care:

- Certain patients, as a result of notoriety or celebrity, may necessitate care provided in a setting or manner that differs from the usual standard so as not to disrupt the care of other patients. In such cases, special care must not result in a lower quality of care for the VIP, nor is it acceptable that it be provided to any patient for nonclinical reasons if it results in poorer quality care for other patients. Special precautions must be taken to ensure clinically irrelevant variables are not considered when prioritizing a VIP for scarce medical resources. If a change in the standard of care for a VIP is contemplated, the patient must be informed, and staff must discuss any potential risks with the patient.

- The cost of accommodating the special requirements of VIPs, such as privacy, security and confidentiality, must not be passed on to other patients.

- Media access, as well as visits by family, friends and associates, must be carefully managed with special attention paid to the rights of the patient.

- Any consideration of potential future institutional or community benefit resulting from the care of a VIP must be carefully weighed against the immediate impact to others.

- Consultation with the institution's ethics committee is recommended. Ethics committees can assist in exploring conflicting values staff members may hold with respect to caring for VIPs, as well as the development of institutional policy and protocol.

VIP patients who present to us for care have the potential to impact our judgment with regard to the setting or the standard of care. It is important that we recognize this possibility, appreciate the ethical conflict and moral distress that may result, and establish proper procedures and protocols that ensure we proceed in a manner that holds true to our values: All individuals seeking care are VIPs.

Originally published in the November/December 2019 issue of *Healthcare Executive* magazine.

Discussion Questions

When might there be a moral justification for giving a patient "special" or VIP care compared to other patients?

How might an organization limit special services for VIP patients?

To Minimize Risk, Ethics Audits Are as Essential as Financial Audits

Paul B. Hofmann, DrPH, LFACHE

THE MEDIA FREQUENTLY REPORT on highly respected companies with enviable reputations that seem to have lost their ethical compasses. Google and Facebook are among these organizations that perhaps need chief ethics officers (Swisher, 2018). Unfortunately, healthcare organizations and their leaders also may suffer ethical lapses and, as a result, face increased business risk. Hospitals have reportedly hired doctors with revoked licenses and failed to report potentially dangerous clinicians (U.S. Government Accountability Office, 2017). Other questionable activities include "cherry picking" patients to increase an institution's quality scores (Phillips, 2018) and making illegal payments in exchange for patient referrals (U.S. Department of Justice, 2016). Even the most prestigious healthcare organizations have been subjected to adverse publicity about unethical or illegal activities (Ornstein & Thomas, 2018; Kolata, 2018).

An ethics audit may not have disclosed inappropriate behavior in such organizations, or even if it did, corrective action may not have been taken. The absence of an ethics audit, however, increases the likelihood that improper conduct will not be identified.

In 1995, the American Hospital Association (AHA) appointed an organizational ethics task force. With the assistance of the Ethics Resource Center of Georgetown University, a six-part ethics survey was produced and pilot-tested in a couple dozen hospitals, many of which then participated in AHA-hosted ethics institutes to discuss the results.

Around the same time, I published the first of two columns on ethics audits (Hofmann, 1995, 2006) for the American College of Healthcare Executives (ACHE), and Thomas C. Dolan, PhD, FACHE, then president and CEO of ACHE, invited me to draft an ethics self-assessment tool. With the assistance of Wanda J. Jones, then president of the New Century Healthcare Institute in San Francisco, I produced a document that has been published annually with periodic revisions since 1997 in ACHE's *Healthcare Executive* magazine and is also available online (ACHE, n.d.).

Although the individual ethics self-assessment tool has found a receptive audience, there is little evidence that ethics audits have gained traction among health systems, hospitals, and other healthcare organizations. Nonetheless, the benefits of performing such audits have been recognized elsewhere.

For example, an ethics audit can help executives "evaluate how well a company has fulfilled its economic, legal and ethical obligations, discover or prevent ethical risks and plan corporate social responsibility activities strategically to satisfy stakeholder interests. . . . [The audit is a] process for evaluating and diagnosing the external and internal consistency of an organization's values and their congruence with real behavior" (Ojasoo, 2016, p. 9).

Unethical and illegal behaviors are not the principal reason for encouraging ethics audits. More importantly, such a process can help identify and highlight endemic issues that have not received adequate attention. Sexual harassment, use of inappropriate language, and other forms of misconduct—particularly by those with supervisory and clinical authority—often go unreported for fear of retribution and increase an institution's potential liability. Furthermore, staff members may be reluctant to express concerns for their safety. In an American College of Emergency Physicians (ACEP) survey of more than 3,500 emergency doctors, 47 percent said they had been physically assaulted while working, and 71 percent said they had witnessed the assault of a colleague (ACEP, 2018). Emergency room and psychiatric nurses, as well as support staff, are also obviously at risk.

A hospital trustee with extensive management and teaching experience identified 63 board leadership barriers as part of a governance quality diagnostic tool (Conway, 2018). Not surprisingly, each barrier has significant ethical and financial risk implications. For example:

- Aims are externally driven and miss internal "losing sleep" issues.
- "Favorites" get their projects resourced; there is no transparency to justify choices and trade-offs.
- Patient and staff harm is not discussed in the boardroom.
- The same types of errors are repeated, without improvement.
- Interconnections among clinical, financial, service, and experience outcomes are ignored, leading to unintended consequences.
- There is little, if any, best-practice sharing or learning.
- No one asks, "Could it happen here?" when a serious event occurs elsewhere.

Frankie Perry, RN, LFACHE, has written eloquently about the kinds of management dilemmas and moral challenges healthcare managers face. In a book (Perry, 2014) that will be published in a new edition in the coming year, she uses actual case studies to highlight why and how these issues demand greater attention.

WHAT SHOULD BE DONE?

Ethics audits are not commonplace in health systems or hospitals at present. However, guidance for establishing them is available, and existing survey instruments can be easily expanded.

The National Council of Nonprofits, for example, published a two-page roadmap for conducting an ethics audit. Among other topics, it describes who should be involved, what should be examined, and how frequently an ethics audit should be performed (National Council of Nonprofits, 2011).

The vast majority of hospitals conduct periodic employee satisfaction and physician engagement surveys, but they usually do not include topics related to ethical issues. As the case statement for the AHA's 1995 organizational ethics initiative noted (Ethics Resource Center, 1995):

> Organizational ethics is intimately linked with personal, professional, clinical and medical ethics. Trust, caring, honesty, compassion, confidentiality and respect are only a few of the essential ingredients that provide the firm foundation on which to base important personal, professional and operational decisions. To be truly successful, an organizational ethics initiative must be internalized at all levels throughout an institution or system and provide open avenues for communication, dialogue, feedback and training. Such an effort takes time and the commitment of the CEO and other hospital leaders to model critical values and behaviors in their own actions—formally and informally. *Ultimately, the effectiveness of any organizational ethics initiative is inexorably tied to the concrete, observable behaviors and decisions of a healthcare institution's senior management and professional staff* [emphasis added].

To assess the ethical culture of an organization, the initiative recommended 55 statements for an anonymous and confidential staff survey. Respondents are asked if they strongly disagree, disagree, neither agree nor disagree, agree, or strongly agree with statements such as the following:

- All employees are treated fairly.

- Respect for employees is important in my organization's policies and practices.
- Organizational ethics are openly discussed within my organization.
- The system of discipline within my organization is fair for all staff.
- The standards at my organization are clear.
- I feel pressure to compromise the standards while performing my duties.
- I know I can freely approach any manager to ask a question about business ethics.
- My senior management acts in accordance with the organization's standards.

Like a financial audit, an ethics audit is simply the first step. What does an ethics audit reveal, and what actions should be taken to address its findings? Physicians and employees reasonably assume the findings will be shared and steps initiated to ensure an ethical culture is maintained and enhanced.

A recent article presented the results of a study involving 3,605 employees of a large, integrated, religiously affiliated healthcare system in the mid-Atlantic region. The study's purpose was to determine whether a correlation existed between employees' perception of their managers' behavioral integrity and being more engaged in their job, seeing their coworkers demonstrate more organizational citizenship behaviors, and having a more favorable view of the service quality of both the unit and the hospital (or other entity) in which they worked. Not surprisingly, there was indeed such a correlation (Prottas & Nummelin, 2018).

Health system and hospital mergers, consolidations, and acquisitions are occurring with increasing frequency (Kaufman Hall, 2018). Invariably, the due diligence process focuses on balance sheets, financial statements, governance and management topics, improved cost-effectiveness, and efforts to preempt concerns about antitrust issues, while only minimal attention is devoted to similarities and differences in organizational culture. Comparing ethics audits as well as financial audits provides additional transparency when assessing organizational compatibility.

No responsible healthcare executive condones institutional or professional hypocrisy, and yet eloquent vision, mission, and values statements are not always reflected in institutional performance and individual behavior. When there is a disconnect between rhetoric and reality, patients, families, and staff are undeniably compromised (Hofmann, 2008). An ethics audit reduces the probability of such a disconnect and helps the organization identify and address deficiencies, just as financial audits are essential in rectifying fiscal management issues.

Given the seismic changes in the healthcare field, it is essential now more than ever before to perform ethics audits to improve performance and reduce liability exposure.

REFERENCES

American College of Emergency Physicians. (2018, October 2). Violence in emergency departments is increasing, harming patients, new research finds [News release.] Retrieved from http://newsroom.acep.org/2018-10-02-Violence-in-Emergency-Departments-Is-Increasing-Harming-Patients-New-Research-Finds

American College of Healthcare Executives. (n.d.). Ethics self-assessment. Retrieved from www.ache.org/about-ache/our-story/our-commitments/ethics/ethics-self-assessment

Conway, J. (2018, July). Governance leadership of quality: Confronting realities and creating tension for change. Trustee Insights. Retrieved from http://trustees.aha.org/qualitysafety/TI_0718_Conway-quality-article.pdf

Ethics Resource Center. (1995). American Hospital Association (AHA) organizational ethics initiative. [Internal report prepared for the AHA Organizational Ethics Task Force].

Hofmann, P. B. (1995). Performing an ethics audit. *Healthcare Executive*, 10(6), 47.

Hofmann, P. B. (2006). The value of an ethics audit. *Healthcare Executive*, 21(2), 44–45.

Hofmann, P. B. (2008). The myth of promise keeping. *Healthcare Executive*, 23(5), 48–49.

Kaufman Hall. (2018, July 12). Hospital merger and acquisition activity continues to rise, according to Kaufman Hall analysis [News release]. Retrieved from www.prnewswire.com/news-releases/hospitalmerger-and-acquisition-activity-continues-to-rise-according-to-kaufman-hall-analysis-300679914.html

Kolata, G. (2018, October 29). He promised to restore damaged hearts. Harvard says his lab fabricated research. *New York Times*. Retrieved from www.nytimes.com/2018/10/29/health/dr-piero-anversa-harvard-retraction.html

National Council of Nonprofits. (2011). Conducting an ethics audit at your nonprofit. Retrieved from www.councilof nonprofits.org/sites/default/files/documents/Conducting %20an%20Ethics%20Audit%20at%20Your%20Nonprofit. pdf

Ojasoo, M. (2016). CSR reporting, stakeholder engagement and preventing hypocrisy through ethics audit. *Journal of Global Enterprise Research*, 6(14), 9.

Ornstein, C., & Thomas, K. (2018, September 20). Sloan Kettering's cozy deal with start-up ignites a new uproar. *New York Times*. Retrieved from www.nytimes.com/2018/09/20/health/memorial-sloan-ketteringcancer-paige-ai.html

Perry, F. (2014). *The tracks we leave: Ethics & management dilemmas in healthcare*, 2nd ed. Chicago, IL: Health Administration Press.

Phillips, D. (2018, January 1). At veterans hospital in Oregon, a push for better ratings. *New York Times*. Retrieved from www.nytimes.com/2018/01/01/us/at-veterans-hospital-in-oregon-a-push-for-betterratings-puts-patients-at-risk-doctors-say.html

Prottas, D. J., & Nummelin, M. R. (2018). Behavioral integrity, engagement, organizational citizen behavior, and service quality in a healthcare setting. *Journal of Healthcare Management*, 63(6), 410–424.

Swisher, K. (2018, October 21). Who will teach Silicon Valley to be ethical? *New York Times*. Retrieved from www.nytimes.com/2018/10/21/opinion/who-will-teach-silicon-valley-to-be-ethical.html

U.S. Department of Justice. (2016, October 3). Hospital chain will pay over $513 million for defrauding the United States and making illegal payments in exchange for patient referrals; two subsidiaries agree to plead guilty. [News release]. Retrieved from https://www.justice.gov/opa/pr/hospital-chain-will-pay-over-513-million-defrauding-united-states-and-making-illegal-payments

U.S. Government Accountability Office. (2017, November). Report to the chairman, Committee on Veterans' Affairs, House of Representatives: Improved policies and oversight needed for reviewing and reporting providers for quality and safety concerns. Retrieved from www.gao.gov/assets/690/688378.pdf

Originally published in the March/April 2019 issue of the *Journal of Healthcare Management*.

Discussion Questions

Ethics audits are more common in non-healthcare organizations. Why are they not more prevalent in hospitals and health systems?

What is the likelihood that healthcare organizations will adopt ethics audits in the future? Explain the reasoning behind your answer.

Redefining Criticism

John J. Donnellan Jr., FACHE

HEALTHCARE ORGANIZATIONS ARE QUICK to laud, with good reason, employees who fix problems on the fly and make things work, all too often in the face of seemingly impossible situations and systemic barriers. Organizational leaders are sometimes less exuberant about employees who point out defects or potential sources of failure in our systems. Employees who repeatedly identify opportunities for failure are often viewed as chronic complainers. Managers may dismiss them as disgruntled persons who are not team players; colleagues may regard them as disruptors to a comfortable status quo. Worse, they may be labeled "whistleblowers."

But in reality, do disruptive complainers do more to fix important system flaws and improve safety and performance? Do leaders have an ethical responsibility to be sure their voices are heard?

In her 2018 book *The Fearless Organization: Creating Psychological Safety for Learning, Innovation and Growth*, Amy Edmondson argues that the degree to which healthcare organizations achieve greater safety and efficiency can be explained to a large extent by the culture of psychological safety that exists; specifically, how safe do employees feel about identifying organizational failure or the opportunity for failure? Edmondson speaks to three types of failures: two that are not so good (preventable and complex failures) and one (intelligent failure) that is not bad at all.

UNDERSTANDING THREE TYPES OF FAILURES

The first are preventable failures, which occur when a person or persons deviate from recommended procedures. These types of failures may be caused by carelessness or malfeasance, but they may also be a consequence of unacceptable or unsafe processes, working conditions or situations. Regardless of cause, we need to learn from these and prevent reoccurrence.

The second are complex failures, which occur when multiple factors align simultaneously and in a way that is not expected nor previously experienced, resulting in adverse outcomes. In a 2012 lecture given at Harvard Medical School, Donald Berwick, MD, president emeritus/senior fellow, Institute for Healthcare Improvement, described his own experience with complex failure.

The lecture, published in Berwick's book *Promising Care: How We Can Rescue Health Care by Improving It*, details how when he was a first-year pediatric resident administering an exchange transfusion, human error and system flaws aligned to cause things to go horribly wrong, nearly resulting in the death of an infant. Berwick describes the shame and self-loathing he felt not only about the error, but how he did not feel safe to speak about it openly, to critically examine what happened and ask how such a failure could be prevented from ever reoccurring. Berwick tells us the experience haunts him to this day but that it affirms for him the ethical responsibility healthcare providers and leaders have to change cultures of shame, fear and silence so employees feel safe and empowered to discuss failure openly.

Preventable and complex failures demand thorough examination via root cause analysis and internal and external reporting. They may necessitate holding specific individuals accountable. We do not celebrate adverse events; they point to significant patient safety failures and have a negative effect on patient and staff satisfaction. But we should celebrate the culture that encourages reporting of failures and the individuals courageous enough to bring them to our attention.

Finally, there are intelligent failures, which occur as the result of well-intentioned, well-considered and well-executed attempts to improve the way we do things. All organizations want staff to continuously look for ways to do things more safely, more effectively and more efficiently. But does the organizational culture actually encourage employees to experiment with, or even think about, ways to improve processes?

Experimentation involves risk, and failures will occur; indeed, failures must be expected. Do we recognize and celebrate intelligent failures as a learning process, or do we place so much emphasis on achieving desired (and maybe unrealistic) expectations that we create a culture in which failure is not tolerated?

As previously mentioned, too often the culture in healthcare celebrates and rewards employees who hunker down and make things work despite systemic obstacles (first-order problem solvers) but overlooks and discourages employees who regularly point out failures or system inefficiencies and offer new ideas (second-order problem solvers). When we ignore or discourage those with the courage to speak up and those with the courage to fail, we send a message about the organization's culture—just not the right message. In reality, the message given is that failure is not an option, and real change may not be what is desired or supported by leadership. The message becomes "be quiet and leave well enough alone." But it is not well enough.

PROMOTING CULTURES OF PSYCHOLOGICAL SAFETY

Edmondson offers leaders some strategies for destigmatizing failure and promoting a culture of psychological safety:

- *Reframe failure.* To encourage more open and honest communication and emphasize opportunities for learning, Edmondson discourages the use of words such as "error" and "investigation," preferring words with less negative connotations, such as "failure," "accident" and "study."

- ***Speak in a manner that encourages open discussions about failure.*** Don't ask staff if they committed or witnessed an error; rather, ask if things are as safe or efficient as possible and if they can speak to examples of such system failures. Encourage conversation that removes the stigma of failure. It is not the case that effective performers do not fail but, rather, that effective performers learn from failure and share what they've learned with others.

Below are additional suggestions for consideration:

- ***Make it clear that identifying and reporting of failures is acting in accordance with the ethical values of the organization.*** Reward employees who model honest reporting of unsafe or ineffective practices or processes. ACHE's Code of Ethics calls on healthcare executives to "create an organizational environment in which both clinical and management mistakes are minimized and, when they do occur, are disclosed and addressed effectively."
- ***Connect identifying and reporting of failure*** to The Joint Commission's culture of safety domain, as outlined in the *High Reliability Health Care Maturity* model and the IHI's *Framework for Safe, Reliable and Effective Care.*
- ***Change the language we use.*** Eliminate the term "whistleblower," and reframe criticism with a label that portrays reporting as a constructive rather than a disruptive activity.

Healthcare leaders have an ethical responsibility to give voice to and reward those with the courage to speak about failure openly and who are willing to risk failure in search of a better way.

Originally published in the May/June 2020 issue of *Healthcare Executive* magazine.

Discussion Questions:

Give one or two examples of preventable and complex failures.

What suggestions do you have for giving voice to and rewarding staff with the courage to speak about failure openly and who are willing to risk failure in search of a better way?

Addressing Disparities

John J. Donnellan Jr., FACHE

THE COVID-19 PANDEMIC HAS made this past year unlike any other in recent memory, as healthcare organizations found themselves treating unprecedented numbers of patients while providing community support and leadership. The pandemic also exposed some uncomfortable but undeniable facts: While COVID-19 has affected everyone, it is painfully obvious that racial and ethnic minorities are more vulnerable.

Most of us are aware of the disturbing COVID-19 statistics for African Americans, Hispanics and American Indians. According to the Centers for Disease Control and Prevention, the number of cases, hospitalizations and deaths within these three groups are all higher than for white people. And public health inequities are not limited to COVID-19. According to statistics from the U.S. Department of Health and Human Services Office of Minority Health and the CDC, infant mortality and low infant birth weight for Black infants in the United States is double that for white infants; Black women are three and one-half times more likely than non-Hispanic white women to receive little or no prenatal care, and they are 40 percent percent more likely to die of breast cancer. Black Americans are significantly more likely than white Americans to have diabetes, hypertension, heart disease and other chronic illness. What responsibility do healthcare leaders have to act when faced with this information?

Three ethical principles fundamental to healthcare are worth examining here: distributive justice (the obligation to allocate available resources fairly and equitably); beneficence (the obligation to assist those in need); and nonmaleficence (the obligation to avoid harm).

LEADERS' MORAL RESPONSIBILITIES

The principle of distributive justice obligates healthcare leaders to allocate resources fairly, to provide emergency care to those in need regardless of ability to pay and to provide a single standard of care to patients with comparable need (as per Joint Commission Standard LD.04.03.07). The principle of beneficence requires organizations to provide health services available to all in need of immediate and emergent care, and the principle of nonmaleficence demands healthcare organizations avoid harm. To help understand their organizations' obligations concerning these three principles, healthcare leaders can consider the following questions:

1. To what extent are we obligated to understand the healthcare needs of the community we serve (justice)?
2. To what extent are we obligated to provide services that address community need (beneficence)?
3. Do we fail in our obligation to avoid harm when community need is not understood and addressed (nonmaleficence)?

ACHE's *Code of Ethics* is a useful guide to answering these questions. Section V of the code speaks to the Healthcare Executive's Responsibilities to Community and Society. In the September/October 2018 "Healthcare Management Ethics" column ("Obligations to the Community"), William A. Nelson, PhD, HFACHE, and Lauren A. Taylor examined the components of this section of the code. A re-examination of that section of the code, in the context of the COVID-19 pandemic, can be instructive:

1. ***The healthcare executive shall work to identify and meet the healthcare needs of the community.*** This demands that leaders gather and examine evidence. What are the public health needs of the community in which we are located? Are there disparities in access to care and health outcomes for those receiving care along lines of race, ethnicity, gender or wealth? Are we doing enough to mitigate disparities that are identified?

2. ***The healthcare executive shall work to identify and seek opportunities to foster health promotion in the community.*** This requirement suggests it is not enough to look only at equality of access and quality of services provided.

   Rather, there is an obligation to consider those services the organization does not provide. What is the unmet disease burden of our community, and does that burden fall unequally on certain individuals based on race, ethnicity, income or gender? Are we meeting that need, and if not, are we taking positive steps to correct it? Do we have an obligation to not only treat disease but also to find disease through health screening and educate the community in disease management and prevention?

3. ***The healthcare executive shall work to support access to healthcare services for all people.*** Nelson and Taylor raise a question: "How far must the work of executives go to support the access of healthcare services to all people?" More than 50 percent of U.S. hospitals are nonprofit organizations with tax-exempt status on the basis of their critically important contribution to the community. Many, especially nonprofit academic medical centers, are located in large, urban settings where surrounding

communities experience higher rates of preventable and treatable disease. In a December 2004 article in *Academic Medicine*, Spencer Foreman, MD, argued that academic medical centers have an ethical obligation to go beyond their classic mission of patient care, teaching and research to also include "building community-based systems of care that are capable of improving the health of underserved populations within their reach." It is advice that is just as relevant today.

4. ***The healthcare executive shall encourage and participate in public dialogue on health policy and promote quality issues, and advocate solutions that will improve health status and promote quality healthcare.*** Healthcare institutions and healthcare executives are trusted and leading experts on health policy, delivery and treatment. Accordingly, there exists an obligation to lend their expert voices to advocate for services needed but not available to segments of the communities they serve.

5. ***The healthcare executive shall apply short- and long-term assessments to management decisions affecting both community and society.*** To truly meet the intent of this section of the code, it is essential that healthcare executives both understand community need and hear the voice of the community. Is the hospital's board and are the strategic planning and advisory committees sufficiently inclusive? Are the persons on these committees in touch with the healthcare disparities that exist in the community served?

6. ***The healthcare executive shall provide prospective patients and others with adequate and accurate information, enabling them to make enlightened decisions regarding services.*** This standard expands the role of the organization beyond provider to that of public health educator. It obligates healthcare organizations to

educate the community regarding unmet need, healthy behaviors, disease prevention and available treatment options.

The preamble to the *Code of Ethics* speaks to healthcare executives as "moral advocates and models" whose decisions affect "the health and well-being of individuals and communities."

To fulfill this role, healthcare leaders have an obligation both to understand and to act on healthcare disparities that exist in the communities they serve.

Originally published in the January/February 2021 issue of *Healthcare Executive* magazine.

Discussion Questions

All hospitals have limited resources. Describe how resources might best be allocated to reduce disparities in healthcare.

The six components of the ACHE *Code of Ethics* are highlighted. Select the three you believe are the most important and explain why.

Addressing Questionable Donations

William A. Nelson, PhD, HFACHE, and Lauren A. Taylor, PhD

TO REMAIN FINANCIALLY VIABLE, healthcare institutions seek donations to foster financial sustainability in patient care, research and education. However, there is a growing recognition of challenges surrounding donations that are controversial due to the donor, the source of the funds or the motivation behind the donation.

To help ward off potential problems resulting from accepting donations from controversial sources, clear guidelines are needed.

POTENTIAL CONTROVERSY

The majority of donations foster little controversy; however, public conversations about institutions accepting "dirty money" raise important questions. Education, medical and healthcare institutions have been critiqued for their acceptance of philanthropic donations from individuals and families whom the public have come to revile.

There have been two high-profile cases recently of healthcare organizations removing a donor family's name from facilities. These precedents inevitably prompt a combination of praise and backlash. The backlash usually comes from people who believe donations carry no moral valence and therefore should never be refused or returned. These views assume, either implicitly or explicitly, that donations are merely cash transfers, and that the important consideration is what an institution will do with the money rather than where the money comes from.

The praise emanates from those who see these arguments as too simplistic and feel donations represent relationships rather than mere financial transfers. When an institution accepts a donation, the act has *functional* value in bringing money into the organization, but it also carries expressive value. Whether the institution intends it or not, many members of the public perceive an institution's acceptance of money as a reflection of a relationship with the donor. The relationship may or may not be controversial unto itself, but the potential for real harm to result from the perceived relationship deserves careful consideration, especially in two key areas.

First, harms may arise out of the provision of celebratory recognition to the donor: Think of the public relations benefits that cigarette companies enjoyed as a result of philanthropic giving long after their products' health harms were known. Harms also may arise out of the provision of influence over the institution: Think of the power donors can command when they are given a board seat or the ability to set severe conditions on a donation. For an institution to take this expressive value seriously is not inappropriate; it represents an insightful appreciation of the social nature of the institution.

GUIDELINES ARE NEEDED

To avoid potential harms or controversy, organizations should have clear guidelines in place to aid in decision-making regarding donations. Such guidelines could be implemented through an identified mechanism that can be called upon for assistance when the development office or institutional leaders have concerns about potential donations. The review body should include development officers,

administrative leaders, board representatives, public relations officials, risk management staff and organizational ethics leaders.

The institutional guidelines should be implemented within a
transparent process. A June 2020 *Cambridge Quarterly of Healthcare
Ethics* article, "Tainted Largess: A Moral Framework for Medical
School Donations," described a moral framework for reviewing
medical school donations, which is equally relevant for healthcare
institutions. The article's authors suggest that when determining
whether to accept a donation, an organization's review mechanism
should consider at least three fundamental questions:

> *What are the donor's expressed views, actions and conduct?*
> If a potential donor has expressed views or has publicly acted
> in a manner that is contrary to the institution's mission and
> values, that should trigger concern. For example, with the
> increasing focus on population health, would the institution
> feel comfortable accepting a gift from an outspoken and
> frequently quoted person who opposes vaccinations for
> children? Such expressions of concern will not always lead
> to a consensus regarding the acceptance of the donor's gift;
> however, the institution should be aware of potential outcry
> when the public becomes aware of the donor's gift.

> *What is the donor's source of funding?* If a donor's source
> of funding is questionable or tainted, such as being obtained
> through illegal activities, the donation may be objectionable.
> Besides illegal sources of funds, there are other controversial
> sources. For example, should a cancer center accept money
> from a tobacco company?
> There will be situations where the controversial source of
> funding is not directly linked to the potential donor such as
> the beneficiary of a clothing manufacturer that closed a decade
> ago following the public exposure of the exploitation of child
> labor seeking to fund a children's hospital. The institutional
> reviewers of a potential donation "must grapple with both the

degree of objectionable conduct underlying the source . . . and the distance removed from that source," according to the *Cambridge Quarterly of Healthcare Ethics* article. It is reasonable, however, that institutions would be less than willing to accept funds from sources that are closely tied to objectional behavior or activities.

What are the donor's motives for donating? When applying the donation guidelines, the review mechanism should also consider the motive and expectation behind a donation. A grateful patient may want to provide a gift to the institution's spine center as a statement of appreciation for the care he or she received as a patient. On the other hand, is the donation being given with an expectation that the donor might gain personal benefits or derive institutional influence?

In addition to these complicated questions regarding whether to accept a controversial donation, there may also be situations when an institution accepted a substantial gift in good faith, yet it was later determined that the donor engaged in morally reprehensible activities or that the funds were derived illegally or in a highly questionable manner. Such situations clearly call for a careful review of the donation.

The review of a potential or an accepted donation is a complex process and therefore costly in terms of time and effort. To avoid situations in which the reputation and image of a healthcare institution suffers as a result of accepting a controversial donation, leaders are encouraged to cultivate and implement morally grounded guidelines for recognizing and addressing such situations.

Originally published in the March/April 2021 issue of *Healthcare Executive* magazine.

Discussion Questions

There is an increasing focus on whether healthcare organizations should accept donations that might be "dirty money." How would you define the concept of dirty money?

What should an organization's ethically grounded response be if it learns that a previously accepted and spent donation was from a controversial source?

Why Good People Behave Badly

Paul B. Hofmann, DrPH, LFACHE

HAVING WORKED IN SEVERAL different organizations, I have noticed otherwise good people behaving poorly under different circumstances. What accounts for this variability and what can be done about it?

Michael Daignault, formerly of the Ethics Resource Center in Washington, D.C., once described why good people do bad things. He cited a long list of generic reasons, but the following are particularly relevant in today's healthcare environment.

- **They do not feel loyal to the organization.** Predictably, this occurs most often among short-term employees and in organizations with high staff turnover.
- **They feel pressure to "succeed" as defined by the organization.** For example, those organizations placing greater emphasis on net income than on clinical outcome, and valuing conformity over candor, are more likely to have personnel who act inappropriately and unethically. Fraud and abuse violations by a number of national healthcare systems and prominent medical centers were undoubtedly motivated, at least in part, by an overemphasis on financial criteria.
- **They feel entitled.** An inflated sense of self-importance and an absence of organizational pride usually contribute to a feeling of entitlement.

- **They believe that the rules do not apply to them.** Just as some people drive over the speed limit, rationalizing that their business is more urgent and they are better drivers than others, there are employees who will assert that they should not be subject to certain policies and procedures.

- **They do not view the act as illegal.** Despite the common perception that an act is ethical if it's legal, the law is usually a minimum standard. In a 1994 *Harvard Business Review* article, "Managing for Organizational Integrity," Lynn Sharp Paine wrote, "Managers who define ethics as legal compliance are implicitly endorsing a code of moral mediocrity for their organizations."

- **They feel pressured by their peers.** This influence naturally begins in early childhood and usually extends consciously or unconsciously throughout one's personal and professional life.

- **They lack resources.** "Cutting corners" to save time or dollars is a convenient excuse for doing something that most people would agree is wrong when resources are plentiful.

Belatedly, there is growing recognition of another pervasive element, indeed an insidious factor, contributing to the failure of good people to do the right thing: bad systems. It may be a truism that a poorly designed, ineffective system will trump a well-intentioned person almost every time. David M. Messick and Max H. Bazerman, in a 1996 *Sloan Management Review* article, "Ethical Leadership and Psychology of Decision Making," noted when an employee acts badly, we tend to contrast him or her with better workers, rather than ask if there is something encouraging bad behavior. If compounded by inconsistent policies and marginally effective computer systems, defective processes can and do complicate the ability of good people to do the right thing.

Actually, when resources are adequate, when controversy is absent, when there is no sense of great urgency, when there are no conflicts of interest and when neither ambiguity nor ambivalence exists, decisions may still be hard, but acting ethically when merely convenient is hardly acceptable. It is precisely during times of limited resources, conflicting opinions, severe time constraints, competing loyalties, significant uncertainty, and potential personal risk that good people are most likely to make and rationalize bad decisions. Unfortunately, denial and rationalization have become useful forms of ethical amnesia.

The relevance of an organization's vision, mission, and values statements should not be minimized in promoting high standards of personal conduct. Similarly, having an ethics officer, code of ethics, sound policies, and comprehensive training programs are all important, but they are not sufficient. Enron had all of these.

Ultimately, as is the case so often, a comprehensive program fostering ethical behavior will succeed or fail based upon the example established by one person: the CEO. If he or she follows Carson Dye's admonitions to adopt a personal code of ethics, to weigh the cost of not being ethical, to tell the truth and not exaggerate, to ensure that actions match words, to use power appropriately, and to admit mistakes (*Leadership in Healthcare: Values at the Top*), then the inclination of good people to do bad things will be much less.

Past experience, however, should remind us of one caveat. Strong leaders can inspire vision, creativity, trust, passion, and pride, but these are not enough. Unless accompanied by the attributes of competency, transparency, integrity, and humility, good people could still emulate a leader lacking a solid ethical compass.

The final litmus test is when staff members, regardless of their organizational status, do not hesitate in choosing the hard right over the easy wrong.

Originally published in the March/April 2004 issue of *Healthcare Executive* magazine.

Discussion Questions

The author mentions the attributes of competency, transparency, integrity, and humility. How would you prioritize them? What is your reasoning or rationale?

Assuming you agree that people have difficulty admitting mistakes to colleagues, subordinates, supervisors, patients, and others, what steps might an organization take to encourage timely disclosure of mistakes?

The Use and Misuse of Incentives

Paul B. Hofmann, DrPH, LFACHE

WE KNOW FINANCIAL AND nonfinancial incentives are designed to encourage specific personal behaviors and to achieve both individual and organizational performance goals. What steps can be taken to avoid or minimize their unintended consequences?

Beginning in early childhood, everyone learns the power of incentives, disincentives and sanctions. Their unquestionable influence shaped our daily behavior, attitudes and decisions. As children our actions were often the result of the rewards, praise, applause, criticism, disapproval, and perhaps even ridicule we received.

We carry these lessons into adulthood and into our professional careers where we become increasingly aware of how and why the proper alignment of incentives at each level of the organization is essential to producing positive outcomes. The type of organization, its tax status, position in the market, form of governance, leadership, and culture all set the stage for either implicit or explicit incentives for both individual and group behavior. Unfortunately, and often too late, many organizations also discover the "dark side" of incentives.

INCENTIVES' DARK SIDE

Without proper alignment and oversight, incentives can inadvertently promote unethical behavior. When results are more valued than honesty and pressure intensifies to generate better outcomes, it is not surprising to witness an increase in unethical behavior. This behavior can be demonstrated in the distortion, manipulation, or concealment of data to improve

- financial results;
- pay-for-performance rewards;
- internal and external comparative analyses relative to finance or patient care;
- public perceptions of the organization;
- job performance of either individuals or work groups;
- support by employees and medical staff for organizational change or CEO decisions;
- budget controls that affect jobs, services and/or physician income; or
- arrangements with private health plans or government payment programs.

Historically, hospital payment programs are a prime example of the power of incentives to discourage efficiency under cost-based reimbursement (1965 to 1983) and then to encourage cutting even necessary costs under DRG-based reimbursement. Similarly, physician payment policies have been criticized for encouraging unwarranted visits and procedures under fee-for-service payment and discouraging legitimate services under managed care, particularly capitation.

But incentives of all kinds remain a popular instrument of management, so it is worth considering what happens when they are used unwisely. For example, unrealistic budget targets, in addition to stimulating possible financial fraud and abuse, may be set too high in order to meet an income goal or too low for the actual volume of work to be done, damaging staff morale and quality of care. Block scheduling of outpatient visits can improve efficiency while lengthening patient waiting times.

If there is an incentive to reduce incident reports, patient and employee safety will be compromised if adverse events are then underreported. When employees see incentives that are counterproductive, unevenly applied, or inadequate, they become cynical about subsequent initiatives.

Sandeep Jauhar, MD, notes in a September 9, 2008, *New York Times* article that too little attention has been devoted to the pitfalls of judging physician performance by surgical report cards and compliance with clinical guidelines. According to one study, the proliferation of surgical report cards has encouraged cardiac surgeons to accept only relatively healthy patients.

Jauhar also references the Medicare requirement that antibiotics be administered to a pneumonia patient within six hours of arriving at the hospital. He indicates physicians cannot always diagnose pneumonia that quickly, so now the overuse of antibiotics in emergency rooms has led to a rise in antibiotic-resistant bacteria and antibiotic-associated infections.

RECOMMENDATIONS

To minimize the unintended consequences of incentives:

1. Build a foundation for ethical behavior. Select the right people for the board, recruit morally conscientious employees, and appoint highly principled medical staff members. Make discussion of ethics a more prominent topic in board, management, and medical staff meetings.

2. Consider the ways an incentive could be abused. Recognize that an employee's need for job security and/or advancement can trump appropriate conduct, especially when this person feels vulnerable or is overly ambitious.

3. Think imaginatively about the full range of potential unintended consequences of a specific program or policy.

Challenge a diverse group of staff members to state what negative developments could possibly result from implementing a particular incentive designed to stimulate only positive outcomes. For instance, is it possible that improvements in infection control or surgical outcomes could be publicized prematurely without verification, or that adverse reports could be concealed, delayed, or downplayed?

4. Make a commitment to complete transparency by sharing information fully, quickly, and factually—an incentive to promote accountability is hypocritical and unethical if the commitment is fulfilled only when there is good news to share. Help board members avoid overreaction when bad news is expressed openly, even if they fear it will harm the reputation of the organization or worry the medical staff.

5. Incorporate elements designed to minimize and discourage inappropriate behavior within incentive plans.

6. Analyze an incentive's positive and negative effects on patients, which may raise or lower perceptions of the organization's integrity and ethics. If families have to endure bankruptcy or forgo needed medical treatment because of a provider's unreasonable pricing policies or collection methods formed by the use of incentives, the community will not be comforted by the organization's claim that "all healthcare institutions do this."

The proper use of incentives can have a positive impact on quality of care and the bottom line. By fully considering all the undesirable consequences of incentives, executives can avoid higher costs and potential embarrassment for the organization. More importantly, patients and the public will be the ultimate beneficiaries.

Originally published in the January/February 2009 issue of *Healthcare Executive* magazine.

Discussion Questions

Of the many examples cited regarding the misuse of incentives, elaborate on three you believe to have the most adverse implications for patient care.

Which of the six recommendations to minimize the unintended consequences of incentives do you think are the most important and why?

Selected Bibliography

Agich, G., and H. Foster. 2000. "Conflicts of Interest and Management in Managed Care." *Cambridge Quarterly of Healthcare Ethics* 9 (2): 189–204.

Asch, D., and P. Ubel. 1997. "Rationing by Any Other Name." *New England Journal of Medicine* 336 (23): 1668–71.

Baily, M. A. 2003. "Managed Care Organizations and the Rationing Problem." *Hastings Center Report* 33 (1): 34–42.

Bean, S. 2011. "Navigating the Murky Intersection Between Clinical and Organizational Ethics: A Hybrid Case Taxonomy." *Bioethics* 25 (6): 320–25.

Berkowitz, K., A. L. Katz, K. E. Powderly, and J. P. Spike. 2016. "Quality Assessment of the Ethics Consultation Service at the Organizational Level: Accrediting Ethics Consultation Services." *American Journal of Bioethics* 16 (3): 42–44.

Blacksher, E. 2008. "Carrots and Sticks to Promote Healthy Behaviors: A Policy Update." *Hastings Center Report* 38 (3): 13–18.

Blustein, J., L. Post, and N. Dubler. 2002. *Ethics for Health Care Organizations: Theory, Case Studies, and Tools.* New York: United Hospital Fund of New York.

Bosco, J., R. Iorio, T. Barber, C. Barron, and A. Caplan. 2016. "Ethics of the Physician's Role in Health-Care Cost Control." *Journal of Bone and Joint Surgery* 98 (14): e58.

Boyle, P., and E. Moskowitz. 1996. "Making Tough Resource Decisions." *Health Progress* 77 (6): 48–53.

Brien, A. 1996. "Regulating Virtue: Formulating, Engendering and Enforcing Corporate Ethics Codes." *Business and Professional Ethics Journal* 15 (1): 21–52.

Buchanan, A. 1998. "Managed Care: Rationing Without Justice, But Not Unjustly." *Journal of Health Politics, Policy, and Law* 23 (4): 617–34.

Callahan, D. 2000. "Rationing, Equity, and Affordable Care." *Health Progress* 81 (4): 38–41.

Chervenak, F., and L. McCullough. 2003. "Physicians and Hospital Managers as Cofiduciaries of Patients: Rhetoric or Reality?" *Journal of Healthcare Management* 48 (3): 172–79.

Cochran, C., J. Kupersmith, and T. McGovern. 2000. "Justice, Allocation, and Managed Care." *Health Progress* 81 (4): 34–37, 41.

Cook, A., and H. Hoas. 2000. "Where the Rubber Hits the Road: Implications for Organizational and Clinical Ethics in Rural Healthcare Settings." *HEC Forum* 12 (4): 331–40.

Daniels, N. 1986. "Why Saying No to Patients in the United States Is So Hard." *New England Journal of Medicine* 314 (21): 1380–83.

Daniels, N., and J. E. Sabin. 2008. *Setting Limits Fairly: Learning to Share Resources for Health*, 2nd ed. New York: Oxford University Press.

Dwyer, J. 2002. "Babel, Justice, and Democracy: Reflections on a Shortage of Interpreters at a Public Hospital." *Hastings Center Report* 31 (2) : 31–36.

Emanuel, E. 2000. "Justice and Managed Care: Four Principles for the Just Allocation of Health Care Resources." *Hastings Center Report* 30 (3): 8–16.

Foglia, M. B., and R. A. Pearlman. 2006. "Integrating Clinical and Organizational Ethics: A Systems Perspective Can Provide an Antidote to the 'Silo' Problem in Clinical Ethics Consultations." *Health Progress* 87 (2): 31–35.

Friedman, L., and G. Savage. 1998. "Can Ethical Management and Managed Care Coexist?" *Health Care Management Review* 23 (2): 56–62.

Gibson, J. L. 2012. "Organizational Ethics: No Longer the Elephant in the Room." *Healthcare Management Forum* 25 (1): 37–43.

———. 2007. "Organizational Ethics and the Management of Health Care Organizations." *Healthcare Management Forum* 20 (1): 32–41.

Gervais, K., R. Priester, D. Vawter, K. Otte, and M. Solberg. 1999. *Ethical Challenges in Managed Care: A Casebook.* Washington, DC: Georgetown University Press.

Goodman, K. W. 2016. *Ethics, Medicine, and Information Technology: Intelligent Machines and the Transformation of Health Care.* Cambridge, UK: Cambridge University Press.

Goodstein, J., and B. Carney. 1999. "Actively Engaging Organizational Ethics in Healthcare: Four Essential Elements." *Journal of Clinical Ethics* 10 (3): 224–29.

Goodstein, J., and R. L. Potter. 1999. "Beyond Financial Incentives: Organizational Ethics and Organizational Integrity." *Healthcare Ethics Committee Forum* 11 (4): 288–92.

Greene, J. 1997. "Has Managed Care Lost Its Soul?" *Hospitals & Health Networks* 71 (10): 36–42.

Grumbach, K., and T. Bodenheimer. 1994. "Painful vs. Painless Cost Control." *Journal of the American Medical Association* 272 (18): 1458–64.

Hall, R. 1999. "Confidentiality as an Organizational Ethics Issue." *Journal of Clinical Ethics* 10 (3): 230–36.

Harding, J. 1994. "The Role of Organizational Ethics Committees." *Physician Executive* 20 (2): 19–24.

Heller, J. 1999. "Framing Healthcare Compliance in Ethical Terms: A Taxonomy of Moral Choices." *Healthcare Ethics Committee Forum* 11 (4): 345–57.

Higgins, W. 2000. "Ethical Guidance in the Era of Managed Care: An Analysis of the American College of Healthcare Executives' *Code of Ethics*." *Journal of Healthcare Management* 45 (1): 43–45.

Hirsch, N. 1999. "All in the Family—Siblings but Not Twins: The Relationship of Clinical and Organizational Ethics Analysis." *Journal of Clinical Ethics* 10 (3): 187–93.

Hofmann, P. 2020. "The Intersection Between Management, Governance and Ethics: Discussion." In *The Tracks We Leave: Ethics & Management Dilemmas in Healthcare*, 3rd ed., edited by F. Perry, 199–217. Chicago: Health Administration Press.

———. 2002. "Morally Managing Executive Mistakes." *Frontiers of Health Services Management* 18 (3): 3–27.

———. 1996. "Achieving Ethical Behavior in Healthcare: Rhetoric Still Reigns over Reality." *Frontiers of Health Service Management* 13 (2): 37–39.

———. 1996. "Hospital Mergers and Acquisitions: A New Catalyst for Examining Organizational Ethics." *Bioethics Forum* 13 (2): 45–48.

Iltis, A. S. 2001. "Organizational Ethics and Institutional Integrity." *Health Care Ethics Forum* 13 (4): 317–28.

Jacobson, P., and M. Cahill. 2000. "Applying Fiduciary Responsibilities in the Managed Care Context." *American Journal of Law, Medicine & Ethics* 26 (2–3): 155–173.

Johnson, K. M., and K. Roebuck-Colgan. 1999. "Organizational Ethics and Sentinel Events: Doing the Right Thing When the Worst Thing Happens." *Journal of Clinical Ethics* 10 (3): 237–41.

Khushf, G. 1999. "The Case for Managed Care." *Journal of Medicine and Philosophy* 24 (5): 415–550.

Lahey, T., E. G. DeRenzo, J. Crites, J. Fanning, B. J. Huberman, and J. P. Slosar. 2020. "Building an Organizational Ethics Program on a Clinical Ethics Foundation." *Journal of Clinical Ethics* 31 (3): 259–67.

Lahey T., and W. Nelson. 2020. "A Dashboard to Improve the Alignment of Healthcare Organization Decision Making to Core Values and Mission Statement." *Cambridge Quarterly of Healthcare Ethics* 29 (1): 156–62.

———. 2015. "A Proposed Nationwide Reporting System to Satisfy the Ethical Obligation to Prevent Drug Diversion–Related Transmission of Hepatitis C in Healthcare Facilities." *Clinical Infectious Diseases* 60 (15): 1816–20.

Lahey, T., J. Pepe, and W. Nelson. 2017. "Principles of Ethical Leadership Illustrated by Institutional Management of Prion Contamination of Neurosurgical Instruments." *Cambridge Quarterly of Healthcare Ethics* 26 (1): 173–79.

Mills, A. 2002. "The Healthcare Organization: New Efficiency Endeavors and the Organization Ethics Program." *Journal of Clinical Ethics* 13 (1): 29–39.

Morreim, E. 1999. "Assessing Quality of Care: New Twists from Managed Care." *Journal of Clinical Ethics* 10 (2): 88–99.

———. 1995. *Balancing Act: The New Medical Ethics of Medicine's New Economics.* Washington, DC: Georgetown University Press.

Myser, C., P. Donehower, and C. Frank. 1999. "Making the Most of Disequilibrium: Bridging the Gap Between Clinical and Organizational Ethics in a Newly Merged Healthcare Organization." *Journal of Clinical Ethics* 10 (3): 194–201.

Nelson, W. A. 2013. "The Imperative of a Moral Compass–Driven Healthcare Organization." *Frontiers of Health Services Management* 30 (1): 39–45.

Nelson, W. A., and S. C. Beyea. 2009. "The Role of an Ethical Culture for the Prevention and Recovery of Second Victims." *Quality and Safety in Health Care* 18 (5): 323–24.

Nelson, W. A., R. C. Forcino, and G. Elwyn. 2017. "Patient-Centered Organizational Statements: Merely Rhetoric? A Survey of Health Care Leaders." *Health Care Manager* 36 (4): 342–46.

Nelson, W. A., P. Gardent, E. Shulman, and M. Splaine. 2010. "Preventing Ethics Conflicts and Improving Healthcare Quality Through System Redesign." *Quality and Safety in Health Care* 19 (6): 526–30.

Nelson, W. A., E. Taylor, and T. Walsh. 2014. "Building an Ethical Organizational Culture." *Health Care Manager* 33 (2): 158–64.

Nelson W. A., W. B. Weeks, and J. M. Campfield. 2008. "The Organizational Costs of Ethical Conflicts." *Journal of Healthcare Management* 53 (1): 41–53.

Nelson W., and G. Wlody. 1999. "The Evolving Role of Ethics Advisory Committees in VHA." *Healthcare Ethics Committee Forum* 9 (2): 129–46.

Paris, J., and S. Post. 2000. "Managed Care, Cost Control, and the Common Good." *Cambridge Quarterly of Healthcare Ethics* 9 (2): 182–88.

Pellegrino, E. 1997. "Managed Care at the Bedside: How Do We Look in the Moral Mirror?" *Kennedy Institute of Ethics Journal* 7 (4): 321–30.

Perkel, R. 1996. "Ethics and Managed Care." *Medical Clinics of North America* 80 (2): 263–78.

Potter, R. 1999. "On Our Way to Integrated Bioethics: Clinical/Organizational/Communal." *Journal of Clinical Ethics* 10 (2): 171–77.

———. 1996. "From Clinical Ethics to Organizational Ethics: The Second Stage of the Evolution of Bioethics." *Bioethics Forum* 12 (2): 3–12.

Powers, M., and R. Faden. 2000. "Inequalities in Healthcare: Four Generations of Discussion About Justice and Cost-Effectiveness Analysis." *Kennedy Institute of Ethics Journal* 10 (2): 109–27.

Randel, L., S. D. Pearson, J. E. Sabin, T. Hyams, and E. J. Emanuel. 2001. "How Managed Care Can Be Ethical." *Health Affairs* 20 (4): 43–56.

Renz, D., and W. Eddy. 1996. "Organizations, Ethics, and Health Care: Building an Ethics Infrastructure for a New Era." *Bioethics Forum* 12 (2): 29–39.

Rovner, J. 1998. "Organizational Ethics: It's Your Move." *Health System Leader* 5 (1): 4–12.

Rutstein, S. E., J. T. Price, N. E. Rosenberg, S. M. Rennie, A. K. Biddle, and W. C. Miller. 2016. "Hidden Costs: The Ethics of Cost-Effectiveness Analyses for Health Interventions in Resource-Limited Settings." *Global Public Health* 12 (10): 1269–81.

Sabin, J. E. 2017. "Using Moral Distress for Organizational Improvement." *Journal of Clinical Ethics* 28 (1): 33–36.

———. 2016. "How Can Clinical Ethics Committees Take on Organizational Ethics? Some Practical Suggestions." *Journal of Clinical Ethics* 27 (2): 111–16.

Sabin, J., and D. Cochran. 2007. "From the Field: Confronting Trade-Offs in Health Care: Harvard Pilgrim Health Care's Organizational Ethics Program." *Health Affairs* 26 (4): 1129–39.

Schyve, P. 1996. "Patient Rights and Organization Ethics: The Joint Commission Perspective." *Bioethics Forum* 12 (2): 13–20.

Spencer, E. 1997. "A New Role for Institutional Ethics Committees: Organizational Ethics." *Journal of Clinical Ethics* 8 (4): 372–76.

Suhonen, R., M. Stolt, H. Virtanen, and H. Leino-Kilpi. 2011. "Organizational Ethics: A Literature Review." *Nursing Ethics* 18 (3): 285–303.

Talone, P. A. 2006. "Starting an Organizational Ethics Committee: An Ethicist Suggests Some Practical and Concrete Steps." *Health Progress* 87 (6): 34–37.

Tarzian, A. J., and ASBH Core Competencies Update Task Force. 2013. "Health Care Ethics Consultation: An Update on Core Competencies and Emerging Standards from the American Society for Bioethics and Humanities." *American Journal of Bioethics* 13 (2): 3–13.

Ubel, P., and S. Goold. 1997. "Recognizing Bedside Rationing: Clear Cases and Tough Calls." *Annals of Internal Medicine* 125 (1): 74–78.

Veatch, R. 1997. "Who Should Manage Care?" *Kennedy Institute of Ethics Journal* 7 (4): 391–401.

Weaver, G. R., and L. K. Trevino. 1999. "Compliance and Values Oriented Ethics Programs: Influences on Employees' Attitudes and Behavior." *Business Ethics Quarterly* 9 (2): 315–35.

Werhane, P. 2000. "Ethics, Stakeholder Theory, and the Ethics of Healthcare Organizations." *Cambridge Quarterly of Healthcare Ethics* 9 (2): 169–81.

Winkler, E. C., and R. L. Gruen. 2005. "First Principles: Substantive Ethics for Healthcare Organizations." *Journal of Healthcare Management* 50 (2): 109–20.

About the Editors

**William A. Nelson, PhD, MDiv, HFACHE,** is director of the Ethics and Human Values Program and a professor in the Dartmouth Institute for Health Policy and Clinical Practice, the Department of Medical Education and the Department of Community and Family Medicine at Dartmouth's Geisel School of Medicine. He serves as the director of multiple courses for Dartmouth's three master of public health programs and medical school, focusing on healthcare ethics. He also is an adjunct professor at New York University's Robert F. Wagner Graduate School of Public Service.

From 1986 to 1989, Dr. Nelson was a W.K. Kellogg National Leadership Fellow, studying US and international healthcare policy. In 2008–2009, he was a National Rural Health Association Leadership Fellow. He is the author of more than 125 articles and many book chapters, and the editor of several books including the *Handbook for Rural Health Care Ethics*. He was the principal investigator of several federally and state-funded research studies fostering an evidence-based approach to ethics.

Dr. Nelson has received many awards, including the US Congressional Excalibur Award for Public Service and an honorary doctorate of humane letters from his alma mater, Elmhurst College. In 2013, he was named an Honorary Fellow of the American College of Healthcare Executives (ACHE) for "his pioneering work in healthcare organization ethics." He has received the Dartmouth Institute for Health Policy and Clinical Practice's student teaching award and, in 2018, was elected to the Geisel School of Medicine's Academy of Master Educators. In 2004, the US Department of Veterans Affairs established the annual competitive William A. Nelson Award for Excellence in Health Care Ethics. He has served as the ethics adviser to ACHE's Ethics Committee since 2006.

 **Paul B. Hofmann, DrPH, LFACHE,** is president of the Hofmann Healthcare Group in Moraga, California. Although he devotes a majority of his time to pro bono activities, he continues to write, speak and consult on ethical issues in healthcare and to serve as an adviser to healthcare companies and as an expert witness.

Dr. Hofmann has served as executive director of Emory University Hospital and director of Stanford University Hospital and Clinics. For 19 years, he coordinated the annual two-day ethics seminar for the American College of Healthcare Executives (ACHE). He is coeditor of *Management Mistakes in Healthcare: Identification, Correction and Prevention*, published in 2005 by Cambridge University Press. He serves on the American Hospital Association's Quest for Quality Prize committee, the Joint Commission's international Standards Advisory Panel and the board of trustees of the Education Development Center. He is a cofounder of Operation Access and the Alliance for Global Clinical Training.

In 1976, Dr. Hofmann was the recipient of ACHE's Robert S. Hudgens Memorial Award for Young Hospital Administrator of the Year. In 2004, he received the Distinguished Leadership Award from the University of California Graduate Program in Health Management Alumni Association. He received the 2009 American Hospital Association's Award of Honor for his central role in shaping the understanding of healthcare ethics. In 2012, he was one of eight recipients of the national Schweitzer Leadership Award.

An author of more than 200 publications, Dr. Hofmann has held faculty appointments at Harvard, UCLA, Stanford, Emory, Seton Hall, and the University of California. His bachelor of science, master of public health, and doctor of public health degrees are from the University of California.

About the Contributors

Richard A. Culbertson, PhD, MHA, MDiv, is professor and director of health policy and systems management at the Louisiana State University (LSU) School of Public Health in New Orleans, professor of family medicine at LSU and a faculty associate of the American College of Healthcare Executives.

John J. Donnellan Jr., FACHE, is an adjunct professor of health policy and management at New York University's Robert F. Wagner Graduate School of Public Service.

Jack A. Gilbert, EdD, is a clinical professor and a Senior Lincoln Fellow in Applied Ethics at Arizona State University and president of Gilbert Associates LLC. He is also adjunct faculty at Mayo Clinic's Alix School of Medicine and faculty at the American Association for Physician Leadership.

Benn J. Greenspan, PhD, LFACHE, is clinical associate professor emeritus at the University of Illinois at Chicago's School of Public Health. Previously, he served as CEO of the Sinai Health System of Chicago.

Andrew Huang, MD, is a third-year neurology resident at the University of Rochester Medical Center in Rochester, New York.

Tim Lahey, MD, MMSC, is director of the medical ethics program and professor of infectious disease at University of Vermont Medical Center in Burlington, Vermont.

Emily C. Taylor, MPH, served as an ethics teaching and curriculum assistant at the Dartmouth Institute for Health Policy and Clinical Practice in the Geisel School of Medicine at Dartmouth.

Lauren A. Taylor, PhD, MDiv, MPH, is an assistant professor in the Department of Population Health at New York University's Grossman School of Medicine.

Cassandra Thiel, PhD, is assistant professor at New York University's Wagner Graduate School of Public Service, with joint appointments in the Department of Population Health at the NYU Langone Health School of Medicine and in the Department of Civil and Urban Engineering at the NYU Tandon School of Engineering.